MEDITERRANEAN
COOKING

MEDITERRANEAN COOKING

Anne Ager

First published in 1984 by Octopus Books Limited
59 Grosvenor Street, London W1

Second impression, 1984

© 1984 Hennerwood Publications Ltd

ISBN 0 86273 134 8

Produced by Mandarin Publishers Ltd
22a Westlands Road
Quarry Bay
Hong Kong

Printed in Hong Kong

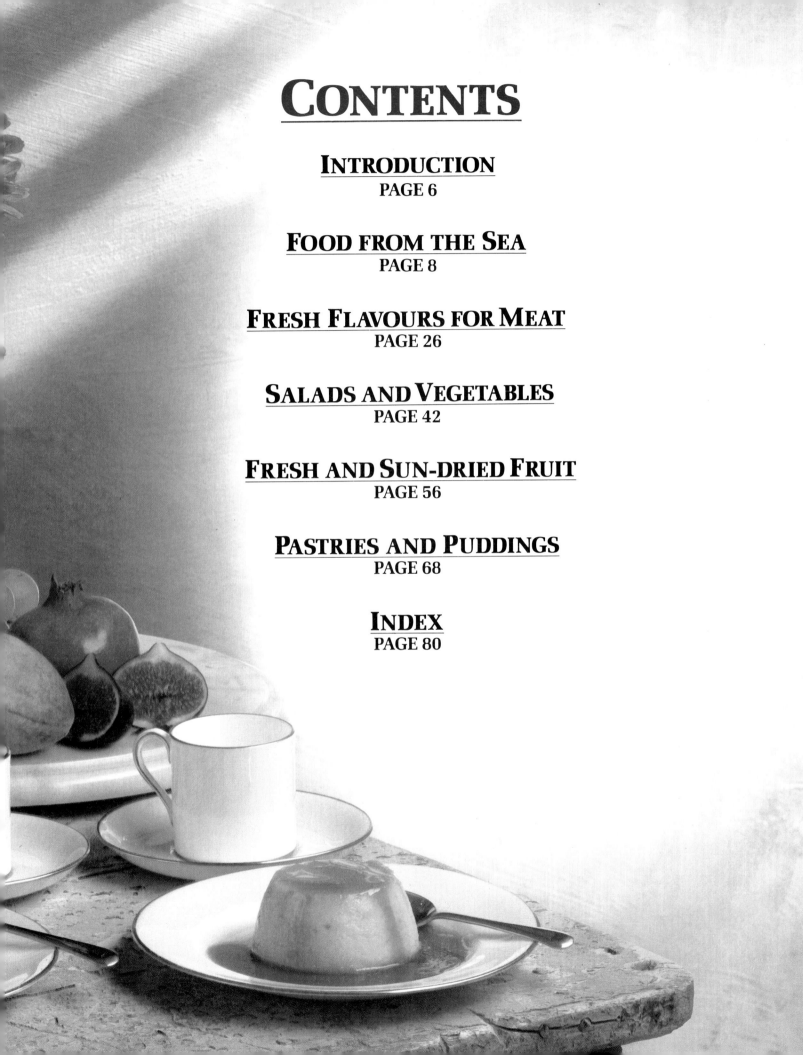

CONTENTS

INTRODUCTION

Food that has been nurtured by the hot sun, freshly harvested and cooked on the spot has a very special flavour, a flavour that is an intrinsic part of Mediterranean food. But enjoyment of these unique tastes does not have to be limited to holidays abroad. With a little ingenuity, a willingness to hunt around for the right ingredients (such as black olives, good quality olive oil and fresh herbs), and preferably some facilities for outdoor cooking, you are well on the way to recreating the flavours of the Mediterranean in your own back garden. For those who do not have a barbeque, most of the recipes in this book can be prepared indoors on a conventional cooker.

Mediterranean food owes much of its variety, texture and colour to the turbulent history of the region. The Moorish occupation of Spain lasted for 700 years and left a legacy of sweet dishes. Similarly the 400 year Turkish domination of Greece resulted in a mingling of Turkish and Greek dishes; so much so that it is almost impossible to distinguish one from the other. The sailors that constantly crossed the Mediterranean from one port to another carried spare provisions with them to swop with sailors from other ships, thus foods were constantly travelling from one ship to another, from one country to another.

The Flavours of the Mediterranean

The countries that surround the Mediterranean have much in common, and yet each manages to retain its own individual culinary character and flavour. It is fascinating, however, that some dishes do appear in more than one country; with a different name but very similar ingredients. The French garlic sauce Aïoli turns up in Spain as Alioli and in Greece as Skordalia. Rouille, the pungent sauce from France which traditionally accompanies bouillabaisse is

found in Spain as Romescu and in North Africa as Harissa. The strength of the sauce varies slightly but it is basically the same sauce.

The South of France Throughout Southern France there is a great tradition of delicious fish cookery: oniony fish stews and soups; simply grilled sardines and langoustines sprinkled with fresh herbs and garlic. The style of cooking in this region tends to be rich, even in its simplest form. The best quality olive oil is used extensively, and the more obscure walnut oil is often used for salad dressings. Goats' cheeses such as Chèvre are frequently used as flavourings in a variety of savoury dishes. Fruits abound, not only in local markets but also in private gardens – plums, peaches, pears and delicious plump fresh figs. These are often preserved in locally produced brandies for enjoying later in the year. In Southern France every market sells large bunches of fresh herbs. The combination of freshly chopped herbs and the locally produced olive oil gives a round richness of flavour to the dishes of this area.

Greece and the Greek Islands This is an area of sharply aromatic smells; the tanginess of fresh citrus fruits is teamed cleverly with herbs from the hills – mint, oregano, thyme, basil and dill. Locally made yogurt is used in cooking as a marinade, as a baste and as a topping. Vine leaves, available in abundance, serve a dual purpose: they are used as a wrapping for food during cooking (as with Dolmathes page 31), and as a 'base' to serve other foods on. The Greek cuisine is a healthy one: Greek olive oil is so cheap and abundant that animal fats are seldom used, and vegetables are traditionally cooked carefully and slowly without boiling, so their nutritional value is automatically preserved.

Spain and the Spanish Islands This is *the* part of the Mediterranean in which to enjoy seafood: freshly caught spiny lobsters, clams, squid and mussels. All are abundantly available and freshly caught. Zarzuela (page 17), a speciality of the region, combines the very best of the local catch. Seafoods are frequently served cold: langoustines with a hot pepper sauce or lobster with a lemony mayonnaise. The seasoning of Spanish food tends either to be subtle or terrifically overpowering: some dishes reek of garlic whilst others are delicately spiced with saffron. There are innumerable types of seasonal fruit available, and they are usually eaten raw, as in most of the other Mediterranean countries, rather than turned into a made-up dessert.

Italy and the Italian Islands Sicily, with its lush crops of fresh fruit, succulent vegetables, plump olives and grapes is the real home of Italian Mediterranean food. Very little meat is produced, but the warm Mediterranean waters abound with tuna and swordfish. The most famous Sicilian creations are undoubtedly their wonderful sweets and pastries.

Candied fruits are used extensively in them, as are a variety of locally produced soft cheeses such as ricotta. Pasta is served with delicious vegetable sauces made with aubergines, tomatoes, pepper and celery. Capers, olives and anchovies appear as the principal flavouring ingredients for all types of savoury dishes.

North Africa This is an extremely mixed area in terms of nationality and religion, and its culture has been much affected by invasions, waves of foreign settlers and its trading history. North African cooking is characterised by the use of huge quantities of spices, certainly in comparison with far more modest British habits. The food however is seldom over-flavoured, as the individual spices are blended with great skill. Cinnamon, cloves, nutmeg and cardamom are among the most popular, as are seeds such as sesame, aniseed, caraway and fennel. Much of the food is cooked in the open; threaded on to sticks or on to a makeshift spit. Whole fish, chickens and larger animals such as baby lambs are frequently cooked in this way, having been basted first with rosewater, orange-flower water or lime juice. Salads of raw vegetables, bowls of fresh yogurt, rice or couscous and a piquant sauce serve as accompaniments. All the North African peoples have a great love of anything sweet – the sweeter the better. Sweet desserts and pastries are not just served at the ends of meals; casual callers and friends will be offered a syrupy pastry or sweetmeat with a cup of strong black coffee or mint tea at any time of the day.

Cooking the Mediterranean Way

The uniqueness of Mediterranean cooking does not rely solely on the freshness of the produce: the way the food is prepared and the way that it is eventually cooked are every bit as important. Along the Mediterranean coast food is frequently cooked in the open air – you can obtain similar results at home on a barbeque. If this is impossible, you can still obtain an authentic Mediterranean flavour by marinating food beforehand and seasoning it imaginatively during cooking with garlic, fresh herbs and aromatic spices. Marinating food for 4 hours or more means that the flavour of the marinade has a chance to permeate the food, and also helps to tenderize it. Do try to use the best quality olive oil for a marinade – it makes a very noticeable difference to the flavour (as with a salad dressing). Try to use fresh herbs wherever possible as well – they have a much softer flavour. As for spices, buy them whole rather than ground. Wine is often a part of Mediterranean cooking. The type used is never crucial to the flavour, but it can lend a special flavour if you use a wine akin to the country of origin of the recipe concerned. There is no need to use expensive wines – all the countries featured in this book produce readily available, reasonably priced wines.

FOOD FROM THE SEA

ITALY

SPIGOLA CON SALSA DI MENTA
Cold Sea Bass with Anchovy, Caper and Mint Sauce

Serves 4-6
1 sea bass weighing 1.25-1.5 kg (2½-3 lb), cleaned
8 tablespoons olive oil
salt
freshly ground black pepper
3 tablespoons chopped fresh mint
4 tablespoons dry white wine
8 anchovy fillets, chopped
10 tablespoons orange juice
2 tablespoons capers
1 garlic clove, peeled and crushed
To garnish:
matchstick strips of orange peel
sprigs of fresh mint

Preparation time: about 35 minutes, plus cooling and chilling
Cooking time: about 25 minutes
Oven: 190°C, 375°F, Gas Mark 5

1. Lay a doubled sheet of greased foil on a baking sheet and lay the sea bass on it. Pinch up the edges to form a deep rim around the fish.
2. Spoon over half the olive oil and sprinkle with salt and pepper to taste and 1 tablespoon of the chopped fresh mint.
3. Lay another piece of foil on top of the fish and pinch the edges of the two pieces of doubled foil together to seal really well.
4. Bake in the oven for 25 minutes or until the fish is tender; test with the tip of a sharp knife. Leave the sea bass to cool in its foil parcel.
5. When the fish has cooled, score down the length of the fish on either side, and carefully peel off the exposed top side of skin.
6. Carefully arrange the skinned fish on a large serving platter.
7. Mix the remaining oil and mint with the wine, anchovy fillets, orange juice, capers, garlic and salt and pepper to taste.
8. Spoon the sauce evenly over the fish, then cover and chill for 2-3 hours Ⓐ.
9. Garnish with the strips of orange peel and the fresh mint sprigs and serve.
Ⓐ Can be prepared up to 8 hours in advance, covered, and chilled until required.

ITALY

TRIGLIA ALLA CALABRESE
Red Mullet with Olives, Capers and Oregano

Serves 6
6 red mullet, about 225 g (8 oz) each, scaled and cleaned
salt
freshly ground black pepper
2 tablespoons chopped fresh oregano or 2 teaspoons dried oregano
2 tablespoons chopped fresh parsley
75 g (3 oz) stoned black olives, sliced
2 tablespoons capers
4 tablespoons olive oil
1 garlic clove, peeled and crushed

Preparation time: 20 minutes
Cooking time: 20-25 minutes

1. Sprinkle the red mullet inside and out with salt and pepper.
2. Fill the cavities of the fish with half of the chopped oregano and parsley.
3. Place each fish on a rectangle of oiled foil and pull up the sides.
4. Mix the remaining oregano and parsley with the sliced black olives, capers, olive oil and crushed garlic. Spoon the mixture evenly over the fish.
5. Cover each fish with a lid of foil, pinching the edges together well to seal. Ⓐ
6. Cook on the greased grill of a preheated barbecue or under the grill until the fish is tender – about 20 minutes. Serve with jacket potatoes.
Ⓐ Can be prepared up to 6 hours in advance.

Variation:
If you prefer red mullet with a really crisp skin, fill the cavity of each fish with the oregano, parsley, olives, capers and garlic, brush with oil and cook directly over a well-oiled barbecue grill.

FROM THE TOP Triglia alla calabrese; Spigola con salsa di menta

ITALY

INSALATA D'ARSELLA E RISO
Mussel and Rice Salad

Serves 6
300 ml (½ pint) dry white wine
1 small onion, peeled and finely chopped
1 large garlic clove, peeled and finely chopped
1.75 litres (3 pints) large mussels, scrubbed and bearded
150 ml (¼ pint) olive oil
100 g (4 oz) Italian short-grain rice
300 ml (½ pint) chicken stock
salt
freshly ground black pepper
2 sticks celery, finely chopped
1 small red pepper, cored, seeded and finely chopped
2 tablespoons finely chopped fresh parsley
2 tablespoons lemon juice
pinch of caster sugar
½ teaspoon fennel seed

Preparation time: 25-30 minutes, plus chilling
Cooking time: 30-35 minutes

As with all mussel dishes it is very important to ensure that all the shells are undamaged and well scrubbed prior to cooking. The easiest way to clean them is to scrub them under cold running water with a small stiff brush. To separate the shells of the cooked mussels twist the two half shells in opposite directions.

1. Put the wine and the chopped onion and garlic into a large pan. Bring to the boil and add the mussels.
2. Cover the pan and cook gently for 5-10 minutes.
3. Remove the mussels with a slotted spoon, discarding any that have not opened. Reserve the cooking liquid.
4. Open the mussels completely; discard the top shells and loosen them from their bottom shells.
5. Arrange the mussels (on their bottom shells) on a flat serving dish. Sprinkle with 2 tablespoons of the olive oil, cover with cling film and chill.
6. Heat 2 tablespoons of the olive oil in a pan. Add the rice and cook over a moderate heat until the rice turns opaque.
7. Stir in the strained mussel cooking liquid and half the chicken stock. Bring to the boil and simmer gently until the stock has been absorbed.
8. Gradually add the remaining stock and simmer gently until the rice is tender and all the liquid has been absorbed, 10-12 minutes. Season with salt and pepper to taste.
9. Allow the cooked rice to cool slightly and then stir in the chopped celery, red pepper and parsley.
10. Make a dressing by mixing 4 tablespoons of the olive oil with the lemon juice, sugar, fennel seed, and salt and pepper to taste.
11. Top each mussel in its half shell with a spoonful of the rice mixture and spoon the dressing over.
12. Cover with cling film and chill for 1-2 hours. Ⓐ
Serve as a starter with fresh crusty bread, or as part of a mixed hors d'oeuvre.
Ⓐ Can be prepared up to 6 hours in advance.

FRANCE

CREVETTES GRILLÉES
AU BEURRE BASILIC
Grilled Prawns with Basil Butter

24 large uncooked Mediterranean prawns
salt
freshly ground black pepper
olive oil
175 g (6 oz) butter
24 large fresh basil leaves, roughly chopped
2 large garlic cloves, peeled and crushed
1-2 sprigs fresh basil, to garnish

Preparation time: 25 minutes
Cooking time: 4-5 minutes

1. Split each prawn by cutting carefully along the belly and through the head and tail, but leaving the back shell intact.
2. Open out each prawn so that it lies flat. Season the cut surfaces with salt and pepper and brush both sides generously with olive oil.
3. Put on to the greased grill of a preheated barbecue, shell side downwards, and cook for 2 minutes. (If grilling the prawns, place them shell side uppermost on the grill.)
4. Turn the prawns over and cook for a further 2 minutes.
5. Meanwhile melt the butter in a small pan and add the chopped basil and garlic – this can be done on the side of the barbecue.
6. Arrange the grilled prawns, flesh side uppermost, on a large flat serving dish. Spoon the hot basil butter over and garnish with the sprigs of fresh basil.
7. Serve immediately with a simple green salad and lots of warm crusty bread to mop up the basil butter.

ITALY

ARAGOSTA FRA DIAVOLO
Barbecued Lobster

2 fresh lobsters, about 500 g (1¼ lb) each, halved (see
   opposite and page 17)
1 small onion, peeled and finely chopped
1 garlic clove, peeled and crushed
150 ml (¼ pint) dry white wine
2 tablespoons tomato purée
4 tablespoons olive oil
½ teaspoon chilli powder
1 tablespoon chopped fresh oregano or 1 teaspoon dried
   oregano
salt
freshly ground black pepper

Preparation time: 15-20 minutes, plus chilling
Cooking time: 20-25 minutes

FROM THE LEFT Aragosta fra diavolo; Crevettes grillées au beurre basilic

Lobsters must be very fresh if they are to be cooked in
this manner; it is preferable to purchase them live from
a fishmonger and to ask him to kill and halve them.

1. Crack the claws of each lobster half gently with
lobster crackers to ensure that they cook evenly on the
barbecue.
2. Put the halved lobsters, shell sides downwards, in a
shallow dish. Mix all the other ingredients together
and spoon evenly over the lobster halves.
3. Cover and chill for 1 hour.
4. Drain off any excess marinade from each lobster
half and place them shell side downwards on the
greased grill of a preheated barbecue. (If you are
grilling the lobsters, place them on the grill tray shell
sides uppermost.) Cook for about 15-20 minutes.
5. Turn the lobsters over, brush the flesh with any
remaining marinade, and cook for a further 3 minutes.
6. Accompany with a green salad.

FROM THE LEFT Trota sulla brace; Impanata di pesce spada

ITALY

TROTA SULLA BRACE
Barbecued Trout with Garlic and Rosemary

2 garlic cloves, peeled and crushed
2 sprigs rosemary, divided into short lengths
4 trout, about 225 g (8 oz) each, cleaned
6 tablespoons olive oil
salt
freshly ground black pepper
finely grated rind of ½ lemon
3 tablespoons lemon juice
To garnish:
16 pitted green olives
16 blanched almonds

Preparation time: 10 minutes, plus chilling
Cooking time: about 12 minutes

1. Mix together the garlic and rosemary and use to fill the body cavities of the trout. Lay the fish in a shallow dish.
2. Mix the olive oil with salt and pepper to taste and the lemon rind and juice; spoon evenly over the trout.
3. Cover the fish and chill for 3-4 hours. **A**
4. Remove the trout from their marinade and drain, reserving the marinade. Place the fish on the greased grill of a preheated barbecue and grill for 6 minutes. (You can use a fish clamp if liked.)
5. Brush the trout on both sides with the marinade and place them other side down on the barbecue.
6. Grill for a further 6 minutes, or until the trout are tender.
7. Meanwhile press an almond into each green olive, then roll the olives lightly in the remaining marinade.
8. Arrange the cooked trout on a serving dish and garnish with the almond stuffed olives.
A Provided the trout are really fresh, they can be marinated for up to 24 hours.

ITALY

IMPANATA DI PESCE SPADA
Sicilian Swordfish Pie

Serves 6
350 g (12 oz) plain flour, sifted
175 g (6 oz) butter, cut into small pieces
75 g (3 oz) caster sugar
3 egg yolks
finely grated rind of 1 lemon
1 tablespoon water
Filling:
1 large onion, peeled and thinly sliced
150 ml (¼ pint) olive oil
1 tablespoon tomato purée
3 tomatoes, skinned, seeded and chopped
2 sticks celery, finely chopped
12 plump green olives, stoned and chopped
1 tablespoon capers ·
2 tablespoons sultanas
450 g (1 lb) trimmed swordfish, halibut or turbot, cut into
    2.5 cm (1 inch) chunks
salt
freshly ground black pepper
3 large courgettes, cut diagonally into slices 5 cm (2 inches)
    long and ½ cm (¼ inch) thick
1 tablespoon flour
1 egg, beaten
1 tablespoon pine kernels (optional)

Preparation time: 45 minutes, plus chilling
Cooking time: 1 hour 20 minutes
Oven: 180°C, 350°F, Gas Mark 4

This is an unusual combination of flavours, but it is a great favourite on the island of Sicily.

1. Grease a round loose-bottomed cake tin, 18 cm (7 inches) in diameter and 6 cm (2½ inches) deep.
2. To make the pastry, put the flour into a bowl with the butter and sugar. Rub the flour, butter and sugar together until the mixture resembles fairly fine breadcrumbs.
3. Beat the egg yolks with the lemon rind and water and add to the rubbed-in ingredients. Work to a smooth dough.
4. Wrap the dough and chill for 1 hour. Ⓐ
5. For the filling, gently fry the onion in 3 tablespoons of the olive oil until soft.
6. Add the tomato purée, tomatoes, celery, olives, capers, sultanas, swordfish chunks, and salt and pepper to taste. Cover and cook gently for about 10 minutes. Allow to cool.
7. Roll out half the pastry and use to line the base and sides of the prepared cake tin.
8. Roll out the remaining pastry quite thinly and cut out 2 circles, each slightly smaller in diameter than the prepared tin.
9. Dip the courgette slices into the flour and shallow fry on both sides in the remaining olive oil until lightly golden on both sides; drain on paper towels.
10. Spread half the fish mixture over the base of the pastry case; top with half the courgette slices and then one circle of pastry.
11. Add the remaining fish filling, and then the remaining courgettes.
12. Brush the rim of the pastry case with beaten egg and place the remaining pastry circle on top. Pinch the edges together to seal and glaze with beaten egg. Sprinkle with the few pine kernels (if using). Ⓐ
13. Bake for 1 hour in a preheated oven. Remove from the tin and serve.
Ⓐ Can be made up to 24 hours in advance.

ITALY

TRANCIE DI PAGELLO COL PESTO
Grilled Bream with Pesto and Tomato Sauce

4 red bream steaks, about 175 g (6 oz) each
salt
freshly ground black pepper
6 tablespoons olive oil
4 large tomatoes, skinned, seeded and chopped
4 anchovy fillets, chopped
3 tablespoons Pesto sauce (see below)

Preparation time: 4-5 minutes
Cooking time: about 10 minutes

Pesto sauce can be bought from Italian food shops and most good supermarkets.

1. Season the bream steaks on both sides with salt and pepper and brush with 2 tablespoons of the olive oil.
2. Cook on the greased grill of a preheated barbecue for 4-5 minutes on each side, putting the fish on a special grid if the bars of the barbecue grill are very wide apart.
3. Meanwhile make the sauce; this can be done on the edge of the barbecue if you have space, or in the kitchen. Heat the remaining 4 tablespoons of olive oil in a pan. Add the prepared tomatoes and anchovy fillets, and salt and pepper to taste (add salt cautiously, it may not be necessary if the anchovies are very salty). Cook gently for 5 minutes.
4. Stir the pesto sauce into the tomato and anchovy mixture.
5. Put the bream steaks on a serving dish and spoon the sauce over. Serve with a green salad and lots of crusty bread.

ITALY

FRITTATA DI FRUTTI DI MARE
Flat Seafood Omelette

6 tablespoons olive oil
1 small onion, peeled and finely chopped
1 garlic clove, peeled and crushed
1 litre (1¾ pints) mussels, scrubbed and bearded
600 ml (1 pint) fresh clams, scrubbed
6 eggs
3 tablespoons chopped fresh parsley
salt
freshly ground black pepper
175 g (6 oz) peeled prawns

Preparation time: 25 minutes
Cooking time: 9-10 minutes

1. Heat half the oil in a large pan. Add the onion and garlic and fry gently for 2-3 minutes.
2. Add the scrubbed mussels and clams. Cover the pan and cook gently, shaking the pan from time to time, until all the shells have opened.
3. Take the pan off the heat and remove the mussels and clams from their shells, discarding any that have not opened. Reserve the cooking juices.
4. Beat the eggs with the parsley and salt and pepper to taste; stir in 1 tablespoon of the cooking juices from the shellfish.
5. Stir in the prawns, mussels and clams.
6. Heat the remaining oil in a *large* frying pan for 1 minute (do not allow it to smoke).
7. Pour in the mixture and cook, without stirring, over a gentle heat until the underside is set.
8. Put the frittata under a moderate grill until the top is set and lightly golden, about 2-3 minutes.
9. Serve immediately, cut into wedges.

FRANCE

BOUILLABAISSE
Mediterranean Fish Stew

Serves 6-8
2 kg (4½ lb) assorted fish (see below)
150 ml (¼ pint) olive oil
2 medium onions, peeled and sliced
3 garlic cloves, peeled and finely chopped
750 g (1¾ lb) tomatoes, skinned, seeded and chopped
1.25 litres (2 pints) water
1.25 litres (2 pints) dry white wine
salt
freshly ground black pepper
2 long thin strips orange peel
2 tablespoons chopped fresh parsley
1 large sprig fresh fennel
1 bay leaf
1 sprig fresh thyme
1 teaspoon powdered saffron
8 slices day-old French bread
2 garlic cloves, peeled and bruised
Rouille:
3 garlic cloves, peeled and roughly chopped
1 medium red pepper, cored, seeded and finely chopped
1 thick slice white bread, dampened with cold water and
    squeezed dry
3 tablespoons olive oil
200 ml (⅓ pint) fish syrup (see method)

Preparation time: 35 minutes
Cooking time: about 1 hour

Ideally you need four types of fish for bouillabaisse: a whole firm-textured fish such as gurnard, monkfish or sea bass; a filleted fish, such as sole or whiting; some small whole fish such as sardines; and conger eel.

1. Scale and clean the large whole fish and wash inside and out. Wash the smaller fish.
2. Remove the head and tail from the whole fish and put in a pan with any fish trimmings. Cover generously with cold water.
3. Boil the fish heads and tails steadily until the liquid has reduced to 400 ml (14 fl oz) and has a syrup-like consistency – 30-35 minutes.
4. Meanwhile cut the large fish into pieces 4 cm (1½ inches) long, the fillets into strips, leave the small fish whole and cut the eel into 2.5 cm (1 inch) chunks.
5. Heat 4 tablespoons of the olive oil in a large deep pan. Add the onions and fry gently for 3-4 minutes.
6. Add the garlic, tomatoes, water, wine, salt, pepper, orange peel, parsley, fennel, bay leaf, thyme and saffron. Bring to the boil and simmer for 15 minutes.
7. Add half the fish 'syrup', the small whole fish, and the fish strips. Simmer for 5 minutes.
8. Add the pieces of large fish and eel chunks and boil rapidly for 5 minutes, then add the remaining 6 tablespoons of oil and boil for a further 5 minutes.
9. Meanwhile make the rouille. Pound the garlic with the red pepper and moistened bread. Gradually beat in the olive oil and remaining fish syrup. Season to taste.
10. Rub the slices of French bread with the bruised garlic, and place each one in a warmed soup bowl.
11. Divide the fish between 8 warmed plates. Ladle the soup liquid into the soup bowls. Serve hot with the rouille.

FRANCE

L'ANCHOÏADE DE LUXE
Anchovy, Almond and Fig Paste

Serves 12
12 fillets canned anchovy (in oil)
12 salted anchovies (in brine), thoroughly washed
1 small red pepper, cored, seeded and finely chopped
50 g (2 oz) blanched almonds, chopped
6 tablespoons olive oil
freshly ground black pepper
1 sprig fennel, finely chopped
1 small bunch chives, finely chopped
2 large garlic cloves, peeled and finely chopped
4 plump dried figs, finely chopped
2 tablespoons lemon juice
2 tablespoons Armagnac
12 small soft rolls
plump black olives, to serve

Preparation time: 30 minutes
Cooking time: 5 minutes
Oven: 200°C, 400°F, Gas Mark 6

Anchoïade is often served as an acompaniment to boiled fish, but this is my favourite way of eating this deliciously pungent paste.

1. Put the anchovy fillets, salted anchovies, chopped red pepper and chopped almonds into a mixing bowl, liquidizer or food processor and blend until smooth.
2. Beat 3 tablespoons of the olive oil into the anchovy mixture, adding pepper to taste.
3. Mix together the prepared fennel, chives, garlic and figs and stir into the anchovy mixture, adding the lemon juice and Armagnac. Ⓐ
4. Split the rolls in half lengthways. Spread one half of each roll with the anchoïade and brush the other half with the remaining olive oil. Sandwich the 2 halves back together.
5. Wrap each roll in foil and cook in the oven for 5 minutes, or over a medium heat on the barbecue.
6. Serve hot, with a bowl of plump black olives.
Ⓐ Can be prepared up to 24 hours in advance, and then chilled (cover tightly with cling film so that the pungent smell does not permeate other foods in the refrigerator).

Bouillabaisse

SPAIN

ARROZ A LA MARINERA
Seafood Rice

Serves 4-6

6 tablespoons olive oil
175 g (6 oz) monkfish, cut into chunks
175 g (6 oz) prepared squid (see below)
1 large onion, peeled and finely chopped
6 tomatoes, skinned, seeded and chopped
2 teaspoons paprika pepper
1 large garlic clove, peeled and crushed
salt
350 g (12 oz) Valencia rice (or small round-grain rice)
900 ml (1½ pints) fish or chicken stock
450 ml (¾ pint) mussels, scrubbed and bearded
175 g (6 oz) peeled prawns, cleaned but left whole
100 g (4 oz) lobster or white crabmeat, in large flakes

Preparation time: 30 minutes
Cooking time: about 30 minutes

If you are cleaning your own squid, buy more than the weight given above to allow for wastage. Prepare as follows: cut off the head with the tentacles attached, just above the eyes, and keep to one side; grasp what is left of the head firmly and pull it out of the body – this will remove the transparent backbone or quill at the same time. Rinse the tubular body thoroughly, to remove the inner milky residue, and slide off the outer skin and fins. The fins and tentacles can be used as they are, the body of the squid should be cut into rings.

1. Heat the oil in a deep frying pan. Add the prepared monkfish and the squid and fry until golden.
2. Add the onion, tomatoes, paprika, garlic and salt to taste. Cook, stirring, for 1-2 minutes.
3. Add the rice and the stock. Simmer gently for 5 minutes without stirring.
4. Lay the mussels and prawns on top of the rice and continue cooking for a further 15 minutes. Remove and discard any mussels that have not opened.
5. Lay the lobster or crab-meat on top of the other ingredients and cook for a further 5 minutes. By this time the rice should be tender and the liquid absorbed. Stir the seafood into the rice and serve with a crisp green salad.

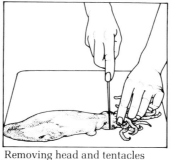
Removing head and tentacles

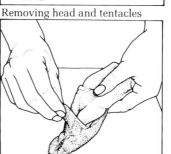
Pulling out the quill

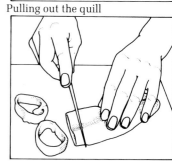
Sliding the skin off   Cutting the body into rings

FROM THE LEFT Arroz a la marinera; Zarzuela

SPAIN

ZARZUELA
Seafood in Wine and Brandy Sauce

Serves 4-6
300 ml (½ pint) dry white wine
2 garlic cloves, peeled and finely chopped
3 tablespoons chopped fresh parsley
1 litre (1¾ pints) mussels, scrubbed and bearded
6 large Mediterranean prawns (uncooked)
1 medium onion, peeled and finely chopped
3 tablespoons olive oil
750 g (1½ lb) tomatoes, skinned, seeded and chopped
1 teaspoon powdered saffron (optional)
50 g (2 oz) blanched almonds, chopped
salt
freshly ground black pepper
1 medium lobster, cooked and halved
450 g (1 lb) sole fillets, cut into strips 2 cm (¾ inch) wide
175 g (6 oz) peeled prawns
3 tablespoons brandy

Preparation time: about 30 minutes
Cooking time: about 30 minutes

1. Put the wine and the chopped garlic and parsley into a large pan and bring to the boil.
2. Add the cleaned mussels and the large prawns; cover the pan and simmer for 5 minutes.
3. Remove the shellfish, reserving their cooking liquid. Discard any mussels that have not opened.
4. Gently fry the chopped onion in the olive oil in a large shallow pan for 3-4 minutes. Add the chopped tomatoes and cook until soft and pulpy.
5. Add the saffron (if using), chopped almonds, salt and pepper to taste, and the shellfish cooking liquid. Simmer gently for 10 minutes.
6. Meanwhile, prepare the lobster. Discard the stomach sac which lies in the head, the grey spongy gills which lie between the tail 'shell' and main body shell, and the intestinal vein which runs down the tail. Cut the meat into bite-size pieces, including the meat in the claws and legs.
7. Add the strips of sole to the prepared sauce and simmer for 3 minutes.
8. Add the cooked mussels in their shells, the large prawns, peeled prawns, and the lobster meat. Simmer for a further 3-4 minutes.
9. Stir in the brandy, heat through, and serve.

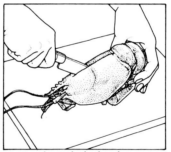
Cutting through the head

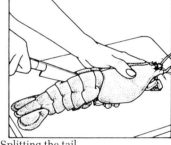
Splitting the tail

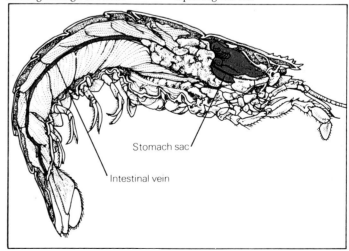
Stomach sac
Intestinal vein

SPAIN

MUSCLOS CON ESPINACAS
Mussel and Spinach Croquettes

450 g (1 lb) fresh spinach
1 large garlic clove, peeled and crushed
freshly ground nutmeg
salt
freshly ground black pepper
1 small onion, peeled and finely chopped
25 g (1 oz) butter
75 g (3 oz) smoked ham, finely chopped or minced
225 g (8 oz) cooked shelled mussels, chopped
3 tablespoons flour
1 egg, beaten
fine breadcrumbs, for coating
oil, for deep frying
deep fried parsley, to garnish (optional)

Preparation time: 20 minutes, plus cooling and chilling
Cooking time: about 20 minutes

1. Discard any wilted or discoloured spinach leaves and trim off all excess tough stalk from the remaining leaves. Wash the leaves and shake them dry.
2. Put the spinach into a pan with the garlic, nutmeg and salt and pepper to taste. Cover the pan and cook gently until the spinach is tender.
3. Drain the spinach thoroughly and leave to cool.
4. Fry the chopped onion gently in the butter until softened.
5. Mix the cooled cooked spinach with the fried onion, smoked ham and chopped mussels. Stir in the flour.
6. Mould the mixture into small croquette shapes, about the same size as a potato croquette. Dip each one into beaten egg and then coat evenly in breadcrumbs.
7. Chill the moulded croquettes for 1 hour.
8. Deep fry the croquettes in hot oil until crisp and golden – about 6-8 minutes.
9. Serve hot garnished, if liked, with deep fried parsley.

Deep fried parsley is a classic garnish for all types of fried savoury foods such as fritters, fish and croquettes. To prepare, wash some parsley, dry it very well and break it into small sprigs. Once all the croquettes have been fried, turn off the heat and plunge the parsley sprigs into the still hot oil. Leave for a few minutes until crispy, then carefully remove and drain on paper towels.

SPAIN

MERLUZA CON SALSA BRILLANTE
Poached Hake in Wine with Fennel

Serves 4-6
1 hake, weighing 1½ kg (3 lb), cleaned
salt
freshly ground black pepper
1 teaspoon crushed mace
3-4 parsley stalks
1 small head fennel, sliced
1 clove garlic, peeled and bruised
2 tablespoons lemon juice
300 ml (½ pint) dry white wine
Sauce:
4 hard-boiled egg yolks
1 teaspoon French mustard
1 tablespoon lemon juice
1 tablespoon white wine vinegar
200 ml (⅓ pint) olive oil
To garnish:
slices of hard-boiled egg, radish and cucumber
black and green olives

Preparation time: 25 minutes, plus chilling
Cooking time: 40-45 minutes

1. Put the whole fish into a fish kettle with salt and pepper to taste, and add the mace, parsley stalks, fennel, garlic, lemon juice and white wine. Add sufficient water to half cover the fish. Bring to the boil and poach gently for 40-45 minutes. Leave the fish to cool in its liquid.
2. Carefully remove the fish, draining it well.
3. Place the fish on a serving dish and carefully remove the skin.
4. To make the sauce, mash the hard-boiled egg yolks into a paste with the mustard, lemon juice and vinegar; gradually beat in the olive oil.
5. Spoon the sauce evenly over the fish. Chill for 1 hour. Ⓐ
6. Garnish the chilled fish with slices of hard-boiled egg, radish and cucumber and black and green olives and serve.
Ⓐ Can be prepared in advance, covered, and kept chilled for up to 4 hours in total.

Garlic is used extensively in Mediterranean dishes, sometimes chopped or crushed, and sometimes, as in the recipe above, bruised. To bruise garlic, put the peeled clove on a chopping board and sprinkle with a little salt. Place the tip of a round-bladed knife over the clove and press down firmly with the heel of the hand.

FROM THE TOP Musclos con espinacas; Merluza con salsa brillante; Besugo con almendras

SPAIN

BESUGO CON ALMENDRAS
Barbecued Red Bream

Serves 6
1 red bream, total weight about 1½ kg (3¼ lb), cleaned
1 lemon
24 blanched almonds, toasted
1 small onion, peeled and finely chopped
6 tablespoons olive oil
2 tablespoons coarsely chopped fresh parsley
salt
freshly ground black pepper
To serve:
1-2 tablespoons capers
200 ml (⅓ pint) mayonnaise

Preparation time: 30 minutes, plus chilling
Cooking time: 10-12 minutes

1. Remove the head and tail from the bream (they can be used for fish stock or soup).
2. Cut the fish into 6 equal sections or steaks. Cut the lemon into 6 thin wedges.
3. Make a small slit in each section of bream and press a wedge of lemon into it. Press 4 almonds into each section of fish as well.
4. Put the fish steaks in a shallow dish. Sprinkle with the chopped onion, olive oil, parsley, and salt and pepper to taste.
5. Cover the dish and marinate in the refrigerator for at least 6 hours. A
6. Remove the bream steaks from the oil and place on the greased grill of a preheated barbecue or under the grill (if the bars of the barbecue are wide apart, place the fish on a smaller greased grid laid over the barbecue grill or on a double layer of foil placed shiny side uppermost on top of the grill).
7. Cook the steaks for about 5 minutes, then carefully turn them over and cook for a further 5-6 minutes until completely cooked.
8. Stir the capers into the mayonnaise and serve with the bream steaks.
A The sections of bream can be prepared in advance and marinated for up to 8 hours.

GREECE

BARBOUNIA ME DOLMAS
Red Mullet Grilled in Vine Leaves

4 red mullet, about 175 g (6 oz) each, scaled and washed
  (see below)
6 tablespoons olive oil
2 bay leaves, crushed
1 tablespoon fresh thyme leaves
1 tablespoon chopped fresh chives
1 teaspoon crushed black peppercorns
½ teaspoon salt
2 garlic cloves, peeled and finely chopped
2 tablespoons lemon juice
12 large preserved vine leaves, rinsed well (see below)

Preparation time: 25 minutes, plus chilling
Cooking time: about 8 minutes

One of the best ways to cook red mullet is to wrap them in vine leaves, which lend a distinctive tangy flavour to the fish. In Greece the entrails of the red mullet are regarded as a delicacy and are never removed; but if preferred the fish can be cleaned before wrapping them in vine leaves.

1. Put the red mullet in a shallow dish. Mix together the olive oil, herbs, peppercorns, salt, garlic and lemon juice and pour over the fish.
2. Turn the fish in the flavoured oil. Cover and leave to marinate in the refrigerator for 2 hours. Ⓐ
3. Remove the red mullet, reserving the oil, and wrap each one in 3 vine leaves; fold one over the head, one over the tail, and one around the middle of each fish.
4. Brush the vine leaf wrappings with the reserved flavoured oil.
5. Place the fish on the greased grill of a preheated barbecue or under the grill and cook for 4 minutes. Turn the mullet over carefully and cook for a further 4 minutes.
6. Serve the mullet, in their vine leaf wrappings.
Ⓐ Can be prepared in advance, covered and left to marinate in the refrigerator for up to 8 hours in total.

Vine leaves preserved in brine are sold in cans or sachets in supermarkets and delicatessens. They are prepared for use as follows: put them into a large bowl and cover with boiling water. Allow the water to cool slightly, then gently ease the leaves apart in the water. Leave the leaves for 20 minutes, then drain and put in a bowl of cold water. Drain the leaves once again and spread them out to dry on a clean teatowel, vein sides uppermost. Once the leaves are thoroughly dry they are ready for use.

SPAIN

SARDINAS EN ESCABECHE
Marinated Sardines

20 small sardines (see below)
3 tablespoons plain flour
about 300 ml (½ pint) olive oil
2 garlic cloves, peeled and crushed
½ teaspoon powdered saffron (optional)
1 teaspoon ground ginger
salt
freshly ground black pepper
4 tablespoons lemon juice
1 lemon, thinly sliced
4 small fresh bay leaves

Preparation time: 20-25 minutes, plus chilling overnight
Cooking time: about 6 minutes

In this country we are not accustomed to eating fried fish cold, but it is well worth trying, especially when the fish is marinated afterwards, as in this recipe.

1. If preferred, clean the sardines, otherwise leave them intact.
2. Wash the sardines and pat them dry. Dust them evenly with flour.
3. Using 150 ml (¼ pint) of the olive oil, shallow fry the sardines for about 3 minutes on each side, until lightly golden. Drain on paper towels.
4. Put the sardines into a shallow serving dish. Mix the remaining olive oil with the garlic, saffron (if using), ginger, salt and pepper to taste and the lemon juice. Pour over the fish.
5. Lay the lemon slices and the bay leaves on top.
6. Cover the sardines and marinate in the refrigerator for 24 hours, turning the fish from time to time. Ⓐ
Serve with crusty bread.
Ⓐ The dish can be prepared in advance but must not be chilled for more than 36 hours in total.

Barbounia me dolmas

GREECE

PLAKI SALONIKA
Grilled Sea Bass with Parsley, Lemon and Dill

Serves 4-6
1 sea bass weighing 1.25 kg (2½-3 lb), scaled and
    cleaned
3 tablespoons coarsely chopped fresh parsley
juice and grated rind of 2 lemons
4 tablespoons olive oil
salt
freshly ground black pepper
4 sprigs fresh dill
To garnish:
wedges of lemon
small sprigs of fresh dill

Preparation time: 20 minutes, plus chilling
Cooking time: about 25 minutes

Although this dish has a better flavour if the fish is cooked over a barbecue or open fire, it can be cooked under an ordinary grill, but make sure that the fish is far enough away from the heat that it does not char before it is cooked. If cooking on the barbecue use a fish clamp to hold the fish so that it does not collapse when it is turned over.

1. Put the prepared fish into a large oval dish. Mix together the parsley, lemon juice and rind, olive oil and salt and pepper to taste and pour over the fish. Cover and chill for 4 hours. Ⓐ
2. Remove the fish, reserving the marinade for basting. Carefully open up the cavity and insert the sprigs of fresh dill.
3. Grease the fish clamp with oil and fit the stuffed fish inside.
4. Lay the clamp over the greased grill of a preheated barbecue and cook for 10-15 minutes.
5. Turn the fish over with its clamp, brushing it on both sides with some of the marinade.
6. Grill for a further 10 minutes, or until the fish is tender – test with the tip of a knife close to the bone.
7. Remove the fish from its clamp, place it on a serving dish and garnish with the lemon wedges and dill sprigs. Serve with Horiatiki (page 48).
Ⓐ The whole fish can be marinated in the refrigerator for up to 8 hours in total.

GREECE

TARAMASALATA
Grey Mullet/Cod's Roe Paste

4 large slices white bread, crusts removed
6 tablespoons cold water
100 g (4 oz) skinned smoked cod's roe or salted tarama
    (grey mullet's roe)
1 large garlic clove, peeled and crushed
3 tablespoons lemon juice
freshly ground black pepper
150 ml (¼ pint) olive oil
To serve:
pitta bread
plump black olives

Preparation time: 20 minutes

This is one of the most popular and better known Greek specialities. Although it is traditionally made from the roe of the grey mullet, it can equally well be made with smoked cod's roe which is more readily available in this country.

1. Soak the bread in the cold water for 10 minutes, and then squeeze it out lightly, without leaving it too dry.
2. Put the bread into a liquidizer or food processor with the cod's roe or tarama, garlic, lemon juice and black pepper to taste. Blend to a smooth paste.
3. Gradually add the olive oil, as for mayonnaise, blending the mixture thoroughly after each addition. Ⓐ
4. Serve the prepared taramasalata with crusty bread and black olives.
Ⓐ Can be prepared in advance, covered and kept chilled for 3-4 hours.

Pitta bread is usually served warm. The simplest way of doing this is to wrap the bread in a single thickness of foil (shiny side next to the bread) and heat it through in a moderate oven for 5 minutes. In the Middle East this slightly leavened bread is often opened up to make a pocket which is used to serve all types of salad in. To make a pocket lay the piece of pitta on a flat surface and hold it steady with the palm of one hand. Insert the points of a sharp, slim-bladed pair of scissors into one end and cut horizontally along the side of the pitta, then gently ease the bread open with the blade of a small sharp knife to form a pocket.

FROM THE LEFT Plaki salonika; Taramasalata; Maaquouda aux rougets

MOROCCO

MAAQUOUDA AUX ROUGETS
Red Mullet Pâté

3 red mullet, 175 g (6 oz) each, skinned and filleted
salt
freshly ground black pepper
150 ml (¼ pint) dry white wine
3 tomatoes, skinned, seeded and finely chopped
1 garlic clove, peeled and crushed
4 tablespoons olive oil
25 g (1 oz) pine kernels, chopped
1 tablespoon chopped fresh mint
To serve:
hot pitta bread
black olives

Preparation time: 20 minutes, plus chilling
Cooking time: 12-15 minutes

1. Put the fillets into a shallow pan. Add salt and pepper to taste and the white wine. Cover and poach gently for about 12 minutes (8-10 minutes for thinner fillets). Leave to cool in the cooking liquid.
2. Remove the poached fillets and drain, reserving the cooking liquid. Put the fillets into a bowl and mash thoroughly.
3. Mix the mashed fish with the chopped tomatoes, garlic, olive oil, pine kernels and mint to give a soft smooth paste. If necessary add a little of the fish poaching liquid.
4. Cover and chill for 1 hour.
5. Serve with hot pitta bread and a bowl of black olives.

MOROCCO

HUT B'NOUA
Red Snapper with Almond Paste

Serves 6

6 red snapper, total weight about 1½ kg (3½ lb), scaled
   and cleaned
2 tablespoons lime juice
salt
freshly ground black pepper
225 g (8 oz) almonds, toasted and ground
100 g (4 oz) caster sugar
1 teaspoon ground cinnamon
2 teaspoons orange-flower water
7 tablespoons olive oil
½ teaspoon powdered saffron

Preparation time: 25 minutes
Cooking time: 15-20 minutes

The stuffing for the fish is rather sweet but it goes
particularly well with red snapper.

FROM THE LEFT Tletas; Hut b'noua; Couscous samak

1. Sprinkle the inside of each cleaned fish with lime
juice and salt and pepper.
2. Mix the almonds with the sugar, cinnamon, orange-
flower water and 3-4 tablespoons of olive oil to form a
stiff paste.
3. Using half the almond paste, fill the cavity of each
fish.
4. Lay the stuffed fish together on a sheet of oiled foil,
pulling up the edges slightly.
5. Spread the remaining almond paste over the fish
and sprinkle with the saffron.
6. Sprinkle with the remaining olive oil and cover with
a lid of foil, pinching the edges together well to seal. Ⓐ
7. Cook on the greased grill of a preheated barbecue or
under the grill for about 15-20 minutes, until the fish is
tender.
8. Serve with slices of lemon pickle.
Ⓐ Provided the red snapper are very fresh they can be
prepared in advance and chilled for up to 24 hours
before cooking.

TUNISIA
TLETAS
Spiced Barbecued Sardines

16 medium sardines
1 tablespoon ground cumin
3 garlic cloves, peeled and crushed or finely chopped
1 teaspoon cayenne pepper
pinch of salt
wedges of lemon or lime, to serve

Preparation time: 10 minutes
Cooking time: 4-7 minutes

Because sardines are such tiny fish, they very easily slip through the grill of a barbecue; if you plan to cook them over a barbecue it is advisable to use a fish clamp or a sardine grill, or to cook them on a doubled layer of foil placed shiny side uppermost on top of the oiled barbecue grill.

1. Split each sardine down its belly; clean the fish if preferred.
2. Mix the cumin, garlic, cayenne and salt together. Rub the spice mixture well into the sardines.
3. Fit the fish into a fish clamp or sardine grill (if using), or arrange them on a layer of foil, and cook over the greased grill of a preheated barbecue for about 5 minutes.
4. Serve piping hot with the wedges of lemon or lime and a salad such as Tzakziki (page 48).

ALGERIA
COUSCOUS SAMAK
Fish Couscous

4 red mullet, weighing 750 g (1½ lb)
2 bay leaves
1 teaspoon crushed coriander seeds
225 g (8 oz) carrots, sliced
1 large onion, peeled and roughly chopped
1 medium green pepper, cored, seeded and sliced
1 medium red pepper, cored, seeded and sliced
large pinch saffron
salt
freshly ground black pepper
1.2 litres (2 pints) water
450 g (1 lb) couscous
1 tablespoon olive oil
2 quinces, peeled, cored and sliced

Preparation time: about 25 minutes
Cooking time: about 1 hour 45 minutes

1. Remove the heads and tails from the mullet and clean them well. Fillet the bodies and cut each fillet in half crosswise. Put the fish to one side.
2. Put the fish heads and tails into a large pan with the bay leaves, coriander seeds, carrots, onion, green and red peppers, saffron and salt and pepper to taste. Pour in the water, bring to the boil and simmer for 45 minutes until the stock is rich and the vegetables are tender. (If you feel that the water is evaporating too quickly, add a little extra liquid.)
3. Using a fork, stir 2 tablespoons of the fish stock into the couscous, then turn it into a large metal sieve.
4. Stand the sieve over the pan of simmering fish stock, and cook for 30 minutes, uncovered.
5. Turn the couscous into a bowl and stir in about 6 tablespoons of cold water and the olive oil; gently lift the couscous with your fingers so that it becomes lighter and absorbs the water. Put the couscous back into the sieve.
6. Remove the fish tails and heads from the stock. Add the halved fish fillets to the stock with the sliced quinces.
7. Place the sieve of cousous back over the pan and steam over a gentle heat for a further 20-30 minutes, until both the couscous and pieces of mullet are tender.
8. Spoon the couscous into a large shallow serving bowl, or into separate bowls, and spoon the fish, quinces, vegetables and juices over. Serve.

Variation:
This is a basic fish couscous. You can add a handful of raisins, some chopped nuts such as almonds, or some chick peas which have been soaked overnight. If quinces are unavailable you can use 2 well-drained, canned pawpaws, sliced, instead. Add them 5 minutes before the end of the cooking time.

Couscous is a fine, flour-coated semolina made from wheat grain. It is traditionally prepared in a couscousier – a two-layer pot with a pan at the bottom for the stew or broth and a sieve at the top to contain the couscous grains, which should cook only in the steam, not in the stock. Couscous is eaten extensively throughout North Africa. The broth usually contains meat or fish and vegetables, but seasoning and additional ingredients vary from country to country. The couscous grains themselves should always be fluffy and separate – never stodgy and lumpy.

FRESH FLAVOURS FOR MEAT

ALGERIA

SFERIA
Lamb Meatballs with Apricot Sauce

750 g (1½ lb) minced lean lamb
finely grated rind of 1 orange
1 large garlic clove, peeled and crushed
1 teaspoon mixed spice
1 small red pepper, cored, seeded and very finely chopped
25 g (1 oz) raisins, chopped
salt
freshly ground black pepper
2 egg yolks
Marinade:
5 tablespoons orange juice
6 tablespoons olive oil
3 tablespoons red wine
Apricot sauce:
1 small onion, peeled and finely chopped
2 tablespoons olive oil
450 g (1 lb) fresh or drained canned apricots, chopped
1 tablespoon chopped fresh mint
150 ml (¼ pint) dry white wine
2 teaspoons clear honey

**Preparation time: 30 minutes, plus chilling
Cooking time: 20-22 minutes**

1. Mix the minced lamb with the orange rind, garlic, mixed spice, red pepper, raisins and salt and pepper to taste. Work in the egg yolks.
2. Divide the mixture into 20 equal portions and shape each one into a ball. Put in a shallow dish.
3. Mix the marinade ingredients together and spoon over the meatballs. Marinate in the refrigerator, covered, for 4-6 hours, turning them once or twice. Ⓐ
4. To make the apricot sauce, fry the chopped onion gently in the olive oil for 2 minutes. Add the remaining ingredients and simmer gently for 10 minutes. Ⓐ
5. Remove the meatballs from their marinade and drain, reserving the marinade. Take 4 kebab skewers and carefully thread 5 meatballs on to each. Brush evenly all over with the marinade.
6. Cook the meatballs on the greased grill of a pre-heated barbecue (or under the grill) for 8-10 minutes, turning them once and brushing with remaining marinade.
7. Serve the cooked meatballs with the hot sauce.
Ⓐ The meatballs and sauce can be prepared up to 24 hours in advance.

TUNISIA

KOUAH
Liver Kebabs

750 g (1½ lb) calves' liver, preferably in one thick piece
24 thin streaky bacon rashers, rinded
8 tablespoons olive oil
2 teaspoons ground cumin
2 teaspoons paprika pepper
½ teaspoon cayenne pepper
salt
4 tablespoons white wine vinegar

**Preparation time: 20 minutes, plus chilling
Cooking time: 6-8 minutes**

1. Cut the liver into 24 equal pieces; roll each piece in a bacon rasher and spike with a wooden cocktail stick.
2. Put the liver rolls in a shallow dish. Mix the olive oil with the cumin, paprika, cayenne and salt to taste. Spoon evenly over the liver.
3. Cover the liver rolls and chill for at least 4 hours, turning them once. Ⓐ
4. Remove the liver rolls from their marinade and drain, reserving the marinade. Remove the cocktail sticks and thread 6 rolls on to each of 4 kebab skewers. Brush the kebabs with a little of the marinade.
5. Cook on the greased grill of a preheated barbecue for 3-4 minutes on each side (or under the grill for 4-6 minutes on each side).
6. Remove the kebabs from the grill, sprinkle with the wine vinegar and serve immediately with Tabbouleh (page 51).
Ⓐ The liver rolls can be prepared in advance and left to marinate, covered, in the refrigerator for up to 24 hours.

Variation:
If calves liver seems rather extravagant, use lambs' liver instead. It can be used in exactly the same way as calves' liver but will need to be marinated in the flavoured oil for 6-8 hours and will require a minute or two longer cooking time on each side.

FROM THE TOP Sferia; Kouah with Tabbouleh (page 51)

MOROCCO

JEDDAD B'LASSEL
Chicken with Macaroon and Raisin Stuffing

Serves 6
1 oven-ready chicken, weighing 1¾ kg (4 lb)
salt
freshly ground black pepper
50 g (2 oz) macaroons, crushed
50 g (2 oz) coarse breadcrumbs
75 g (3 oz) raisins
1 tablespoon chopped fresh basil
1 egg, beaten
4 tablespoons olive oil
3 tablespoons honey, melted
1 tablespoon lemon juice
1 teaspoon ground cinnamon

Preparation time: 15 minutes
Cooking time: 1½-1¾ hours

This is one of the most unusual ways I have come across for cooking a whole chicken; although the stuffing is rather sweet, the overall combination of flavours is absolutely delicious.

1. Rub the bird inside and out with salt and pepper.
2. Mix together the crushed macaroons, breadcrumbs, raisins, chopped basil, beaten egg and salt and pepper to taste. Stuff the chicken with this mixture and secure the opening with small metal skewers.
3. Rub olive oil all over the stuffed chicken. Fix the chicken securely on a spit, and roast over a preheated barbecue (or in the oven) for 45 minutes.
4. Mix the melted honey with the lemon juice and brush the chicken all over, then sprinkle with the ground cinnamon. Continue roasting on the spit for a further 45 minutes; then test to check that the chicken is done by pricking the thickest part with a fine skewer. If the juices run red, continue cooking for another 10 minutes.
5. Serve hot with Tabbouleh (page 51).

ALGERIA/MOROCCO

MECHOUI
Spit-roasted Lamb

Serves 6-8
1 leg of lamb, weighing 2 kg (4¾ lb)
Marinade:
150 ml (¼ pint) olive oil
1 tablespoon chopped fresh marjoram
2 tablespoons chopped fresh mint
½ teaspoon ground cinnamon
½ teaspoon ground cloves
2 cloves garlic, peeled and crushed
salt
freshly ground black pepper
2 tablespoons rosewater (for sprinkling during cooking)

Preparation time: 10 minutes, plus chilling
Cooking time: 40-50 minutes for the first slices (see below)

I first ate Mechoui in the Algerian Sahara, an experience that I have never forgotten; a whole baby lamb, sprinkled with rosewater, was roasted steadily on a spit. Not many of us have a spit large enough to take a whole lamb, so the recipe here is for just a leg. Cook it on a rotating spit over a barbecue – the first slices should be ready to cut and serve within 35-45 minutes, and the meat will continue to cook whilst the first slices are being enjoyed. This recipe really does need to be spit-roasted, but you can use an oven spit rather than one attached to a barbecue.

1. With a small sharp knife, make several deep widthways cuts at regular intervals in the leg of lamb. Put the lamb into a shallow dish.
2. Mix the marinade ingredients together and spoon evenly over the lamb; cover the lamb and chill for at least 6 hours, turning it from time to time. Ⓐ
3. Remove the lamb from its marinade and drain, reserving the marinade. Fix the joint securely on to the spit and brush all over with a little of the marinade.
4. Spit-roast over the preheated barbecue for about 35-45 minutes until the lamb is sufficiently cooked to carve off the outer slices. Leave the rest of the lamb on the spit and carve off slices as they are ready.
5. Serve with warm pitta bread and a cucumber and yoghurt salad.
Ⓐ The lamb has an even more delicious flavour if it is marinated for 24 hours in the refrigerator before cooking.

> Rosewater is used as a flavouring for lamb, poultry and sweet dishes. It can be bought from most chemists or made at home. To make rosewater put 225 g (8 oz) unblemished red rose leaves in a pan with 450 ml (¾ pint) water. Simmer steadily for about 30 minutes until all the water has been drawn out of the leaves and they have become limp. Strain the rose-coloured liquid into a clean pan, add 75 g (3 oz) sugar and stir until dissolved. Simmer for 5 minutes then cool. Store in a screw-topped jar in the refrigerator for up to 2 weeks.

FROM THE TOP Mechoui; Quodban

MOROCCO

QUODBAN
Spiced Lamb Kebabs

750 g (1½ lb) lamb fillet
2 tablespoons lemon juice
150 ml (¼ pint) olive oil
2 teaspoons crushed coriander seeds
2 garlic cloves, peeled and crushed
2 teaspoons ground turmeric
1 teaspoon ground ginger
2 teaspoons ground cumin
2 bay leaves, crumbled
salt
freshly ground black pepper
2 limes, cut into thin wedges
hot pitta bread, to serve

Preparation time: 20-25 minutes, plus chilling
Cooking time: 5-8 minutes.

1. Trim off any fat or sinew from the lamb and cut it into 2.5 cm (1 inch) cubes.
2. Put the cubed meat into a shallow dish. Mix the lemon juice with the olive oil, crushed coriander seeds, garlic, turmeric, ginger, cumin, crumbled bay leaves and salt and pepper to taste. Pour this marinade over the meat and stir well.
3. Cover the meat and chill for 12 hours, turning the cubes once or twice. Ⓐ
4. Remove the meat and drain, reserving the marinade. Thread the cubes of meat on to 4 kebab skewers, threading wedges of lime in between some of the cubes. Brush each kebab with some of the marinade.
5. Cook the kebabs on the greased grill of a preheated barbecue (or under the grill) for 5-8 minutes, until the meat is cooked.
6. Serve the kebabs with hot pitta bread.
Ⓐ The kebabs can be prepared in advance, covered, and left to marinate in the refrigerator for up to 24 hours.

GREECE

KOTOPOULO LEMONATO
Chicken in Lemon and Basil Sauce

50 g (2 oz) butter
2 tablespoons olive oil
4 chicken quarters
1 medium onion, peeled and thinly sliced
2 large carrots, peeled and roughly chopped
2 sticks celery, chopped
1 large sprig fresh basil (with at least 8 good-sized leaves),
  chopped
6 tablespoons lemon juice
salt
freshly ground black pepper
150 ml (¼ pint) chicken stock
2 tablespoons chopped fresh parsley, to garnish

Preparation time: 10 minutes
Cooking time: 1-1¼ hours

The secret of this recipe lies in using really sharp juicy lemons and fresh basil.

1. Heat the butter and olive oil in a large deep frying pan. Add the chicken quarters and fry until lightly golden on all sides. Remove the chicken with a slotted spoon.
2. Add the onion, carrots and celery to the pan and fry gently for 5 minutes.
3. Return the chicken to the pan, together with the basil, lemon juice and salt and pepper to taste. Cook steadily until all the juice has evaporated.
4. Add the chicken stock and simmer gently, covered, for about 45 minutes-1 hour until tender. F
5. Sprinkle with the chopped parsley and serve, accompanied by noodles or plain boiled potatoes.
F Freeze for up to 1 month. Thaw in the refrigerator for 6-8 hours. Reheat in a saucepan over a moderate heat.

Variation:
The flavour is just as delicious if joints of tame rabbit are used in place of chicken quarters. Use in exactly the same way.

FROM THE LEFT Kotopoulo lemonato; Dolmathes

GREECE

DOLMATHES
Stuffed Vine Leaves

Serves 5-6

110 g (4 oz) long-grain rice
salt
500 g (1¼ lb) finely minced lean beef or lamb
5 spring onions, finely chopped
1½ tablespoons chopped fresh dill
3-4 tablespoons chopped fresh parsley
grated rind of ½ lemon
1 egg white, stiffly beaten
2 tablespoons pine kernels, chopped
freshly ground black pepper
225 g (8 oz) prepared vine leaves (see page 20)
450 ml (¾ pint) chicken stock
150 ml (¼ pint) dry white wine
Sauce:
3 egg yolks
2 tablespoons lemon juice
1 tablespoon cornflour
250 ml (8 fl oz) cooking liquid from the dolmathes

Preparation time: 45 minutes
Cooking time: 60-70 minutes

1. Cook the rice in boiling salted water for 5 minutes; drain thoroughly.
2. Mix the rice with the minced meat, spring onions, dill, parsley, lemon rind, egg white, pine kernels, and salt and pepper to taste.
3. Line the base of a large deep frying pan with 4-5 vine leaves; reserve 4 leaves for serving.
4. Divide the prepared rice and meat filling between the remaining vine leaves, shaping each portion into a small sausage.
5. Fold over the stem end of each vine leaf; fold both edges of each leaf into the middle, and roll the leaf up to make a neat 'sausage'.
6. Lay the rolled dolmathes fairly closely together in the frying pan, arranging them in 2 layers if necessary.
7. Add salt, pepper, and the stock and white wine to the pan. Cover and simmer gently for 50-60 minutes. ⬚F
8. Meanwhile, whisk the egg yolks with the lemon juice and cornflour, ready for the sauce.
9. Once the dolmathes are cooked, strain off the cooking liquid and reserve 250 ml (8 fl oz). ⬚F Lay the reserved vine leaves on a serving dish, arrange the dolmathes on top and keep warm.
10. Whisk 4 tablespoons of the reserved cooking liquid into the egg yolk mixture, then whisk in the remaining reserved cooking liquid.
11. Transfer to a saucepan and stir over a gentle heat until the sauce thickens; do not allow the sauce to boil rapidly.
12. Spoon some of the sauce over the dolmathes, and serve the remaining sauce separately.

⬚F Freeze for up to 1 month. Freeze cooking liquid separately. Thaw at room temperature for 4 hours then heat dolmathes and cooking liquid through and proceed.

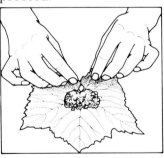
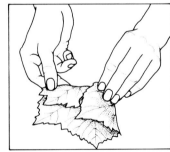
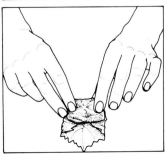

1. Folding over the stem
2. Folding in the edges
3. Rolling the leaf up

ITALY

BISTECCA ALLA PIZZAIOLA
Steak with Tomato and Red Wine Sauce

1 piece sirloin or porterhouse steak, about 1 kg (2 lb)
6 tablespoons olive oil
1 tablespoon chopped fresh oregano
1 large garlic clove, peeled and crushed
salt
freshly ground black pepper
Sauce:
1 small onion, peeled and finely chopped
2 tablespoons olive oil
750 g (1½ lb) tomatoes, skinned, seeded and chopped
6 tablespoons chopped fresh oregano
2 garlic cloves, peeled and crushed
6 tablespoons full-bodied red wine

Preparation time: 10 minutes, plus chilling
Cooking time: about 45 minutes (see recipe)

For a perfect result the piece of steak should be about 5 cm (2 inches) thick. This is one recipe that really should be cooked over the barbecue.

1. Put the steak into a shallow dish. Mix the olive oil with the oregano, garlic and salt and pepper to taste. Spoon the marinade over the meat.
2. Cover the steak and chill thoroughly for 4-6 hours, turning once. Ⓐ
3. To make the sauce, gently fry the onion in the olive oil for 3-4 minutes. Add the tomatoes, oregano, garlic and red wine, and simmer for 10 minutes. Ⓐ
4. Remove the steak from its marinade and drain, reserving the marinade. Place on the greased grill of a preheated barbecue and cook for about 15 minutes for a medium steak, increasing or decreasing the cooking time according to how you like your steak cooked. Turn the steak over, brush with some of the marinade and cook for the same length of time on the other side.
5. To serve, cut the steak into thickish slices and top each portion with some of the hot sauce.
Ⓐ The steak can be prepared in advance and left to marinate, covered, for up to 12 hours. The sauce can be prepared up to 12 hours in advance also, covered and kept chilled.

FROM THE TOP Moussaka; Souvlakia

GREECE

MOUSSAKA
Aubergine and Lamb Pie

Serves 6
1 kg (2¼ lb) aubergines
salt
150 ml (¼ pint) olive or cooking oil, for frying
75 g (3 oz) Kefalotyri or Parmesan cheese, grated
3 tablespoons crisp dry breadcrumbs
Meat filling:
1 large onion, peeled and finely chopped
2 tablespoons olive or cooking oil
500 g (1¼ lb) lean minced lamb
450 g (1 lb) tomatoes, roughly chopped
2 tablespoons tomato purée
150 ml (¼ pint) dry white wine
1 tablespoon chopped fresh oregano or fresh basil
large pinch of ground nutmeg
large pinch of ground cinnamon
salt
freshly ground black pepper
75 g (3 oz) Kefalotyri or Parmesan cheese, grated
Sauce:
600 ml (1 pint) milk
small piece of stick cinnamon
1 bay leaf
55 g (2 oz) butter
55 g (2 oz) plain flour

Preparation time: about 30 minutes, plus standing
Cooking time: about 1 hour 35 minutes
Oven: 180°C, 350°F, Gas Mark 4

1. Top and tail the aubergines; cut them into ½ cm (¼ inch) slices. Put the slices into a large bowl of well-salted water and leave to stand for 30 minutes.
2. Squeeze the aubergine slices gently, then rinse in cold running water; squeeze them again and leave in a colander lined with a tea-towel for 1 hour.
3. Meanwhile make the meat filling: fry the onion gently in the oil for 2-3 minutes. Add the lamb and cook until lightly browned. Add the tomatoes, tomato purée, wine, oregano or basil, nutmeg, cinnamon, and salt and pepper. Simmer gently for 30 minutes.
4. Shallow fry the drained aubergine slices in the oil on both sides until lightly golden. (You will probably need to do this in about 3 batches.) Drain the slices thoroughly on paper towels.
5. Stir the cheese into the meat filling.
6. Spoon half the meat filling into a large, lightly greased gratin dish; lay half the fried aubergine slices on top. Add the remaining meat filling, then arrange the remaining aubergine slices on top.
7. To make the sauce, heat the milk in a pan with the cinnamon stick and bay leaf; put to one side.
8. Heat the butter in a pan and stir in the flour. Gradually stir in the strained milk, beating well. Simmer without stirring for 2-3 minutes.
9. Spoon the sauce evenly over the moussaka and sprinkle with the cheese and breadcrumbs. F A
10. Bake in the oven for 1 hour until the top of the moussaka is crisp and golden.
11. Serve piping hot with a crisp salad.
F Can be frozen for up to 6 months. Cook from frozen for 1¼ hours.
A Can be prepared up to 24 hours in advance.

GREECE

SOUVLAKIA
Lamb and Feta Kebabs

1 kg (2 lb) lean lamb, cut into 4 cm (1½ inch) cubes.
6 tablespoons olive oil
4 tablespoons lemon juice
2 large garlic cloves, peeled and crushed
1 tablespoon chopped fresh oregano
1 tablespoon chopped fresh thyme
1 tablespoon chopped fresh marjoram
salt
freshly ground black pepper
To serve:
100 g (4 oz) Feta cheese, crumbled
4 bay leaves, crumbled (optional)
pitta bread

Preparation time: 25 minutes, plus chilling
Cooking time: about 10 minutes

1. Trim any fat or sinew from the lamb cubes and put them in a shallow dish. Mix the olive oil with the lemon juice, garlic, chopped herbs and salt and pepper to taste. Spoon this marinade evenly over the lamb.
2. Cover the dish and chill for at least 4 hours. A
3. Remove the lamb cubes and drain, reserving the marinade. Thread the cubes on to 4 kebab skewers and brush with some of the marinade.
4. Cook on the greased grill of a preheated barbecue (or under the grill) for about 5 minutes on each side.
5. Sprinkle the kebabs with the crumbled Feta cheese (and the crumbled bay leaves, if liked). Serve immediately with pitta bread and a vegetable dish such as Patates Latheres me Lemoni (page 50).
A The lamb cubes can be marinated for up to 24 hours in total.

ITALY

POLLO PISTO
Marinated Chicken with Mushroom and Marsala Sauce

4 large unboned chicken breasts
5 tablespoons lemon juice
6 tablespoons olive oil
1 tablespoon chopped fresh rosemary
salt
freshly ground black pepper
Sauce:
25 g (1 oz) butter
2 tablespoons olive oil
1 medium onion, peeled and finely chopped
1 garlic clove, peeled and crushed
3 rashers lean bacon, rinded and finely chopped
100 g (4 oz) button mushrooms, sliced
50 g (2 oz) chicken livers, chopped
1 tablespoon flour
200 ml (⅓ pint) red wine
4 tablespoons Marsala

**Preparation time: 10 minutes, plus chilling
Cooking time: about 35 minutes.**

1. Put the chicken breasts in a shallow dish. Mix the lemon juice with the olive oil, rosemary and salt and pepper to taste, and spoon evenly over the chicken. Cover and chill for 3-4 hours, turning the chicken once. **A**
2. Then make the sauce. Heat the butter and oil in a pan, add the onion, garlic and bacon and fry gently for 5 minutes. Add the mushrooms and chicken livers and cook for a further 2 minutes. Stir in the flour, then gradually add the red wine and Marsala. Simmer the sauce for about 15 minutes. **A**
3. Remove the chicken breasts from their marinade and drain, reserving the marinade. Brush the non-skin side with a little of the marinade and place that side down on the greased grill of a preheated barbecue. Cook for 7 minutes. (The chicken breasts can also be grilled, the other way up, for the same length of time.)
4. Brush both sides of the chicken breasts with the marinade and place skin side down on the barbecue (skin side up if grilling); cook for a further 3-5 minutes until tender.
5. Serve with the hot sauce, a tossed salad, and plenty of crusty bread.
A The chicken breasts can be prepared in advance and left to marinate, covered, in the refrigerator for up to 12 hours. The sauce can be prepared up to 24 hours in advance, covered and kept chilled. Reheat on the side of the barbecue when needed.

FROM THE TOP Pollo pisto; Picadillo Andaluzia

SPAIN

PICADILLO ANDALUZIA
Skewered Meatballs with Pepper, Olive and Nut Sauce

Serves 6
1 kg (2¼ lb) good quality minced beef
1 medium onion, peeled and finely chopped
1 garlic clove, peeled and crushed
¼ teaspoon chilli powder
salt
freshly ground black pepper
30 blanched almonds
oil, for brushing
Sauce:
2 tablespoons olive oil
1 small onion, peeled and finely chopped
450 g (1 lb) tomatoes, skinned, seeded and chopped
2 tablespoons tomato purée
1 large garlic clove, peeled and crushed
1 eating apple, cored and grated
300 ml (½ pint) red wine
150 ml (¼ pint) dry sherry
2 small fresh red chilli peppers, finely chopped
25 g (1 oz) raisins
½ teaspoon ground cinnamon
salt
freshly ground black pepper
50 g (2 oz) stuffed olives, sliced
1 tablespoon chopped blanched almonds

**Preparation time: 20-25 minutes
Cooking time: 17-20 minutes**

Buy really good quality lean mince from your butcher for these meatballs; the better the meat and the finer it is minced, the better the meatballs you will be able to serve from your barbecue. If you do not have a barbecue, grill the meatballs under a moderately hot grill for 5-8 minutes, turning once.

1. Mix the minced beef with the onion, garlic, chilli powder and salt and pepper to taste, working the ingredients together until they are thoroughly mixed.
2. Divide the meat mixture into 30 equal portions and shape each one into a ball; press a whole almond into the centre of each meatball. Chill for 4 hours.
3. For the sauce, heat the oil in a large saucepan and fry the onion gently for 3 minutes. Add all the remaining sauce ingredients, except the olives and almonds, and cook steadily for 6-7 minutes.
4. Stir in the olives and almonds. Cover the pan and keep warm on the side of the barbecue.
5. Take 6 skewers and thread 5 meatballs on to each. Brush on all sides with oil.
6. Cook the meatballs on the greased grill of a pre-heated barbecue for 8-10 minutes, turning once.
7. Serve the cooked meatballs with the hot sauce.

ITALY

SCALOPPINE AL FONTINA E SALVIA
Veal and Fontina Cheese Rolls

Serves 6
75 g (3 oz) unsalted butter, softened
2 tablespoons chopped fresh parsley
1 tablespoon chopped fresh sage
1 garlic clove, peeled and crushed
finely grated rind of 1 lemon
salt
freshly ground black pepper
6 long thin veal escalopes, total weight about 500 g (1¼ lb)
6 thin slices Parma ham
6 very thin slices Fontina or Mozzarella cheese, total
   weight about 175 g (6 oz)
4 tablespoons olive oil, for brushing
Aïoli di Marsala:
2 garlic cloves, peeled and crushed
2 teaspoons Dijon mustard
1 teaspoon lemon juice
2 egg yolks
200 ml (⅓ pint) olive oil
salt
freshly ground black pepper
2 tablespoons Marsala
To garnish:
fresh sage leaves
lemon slices

Preparation time: 45 minutes, plus chilling overnight
Cooking time: 8-10 minutes

These veal rolls have a better flavour when cooked over the barbecue, but if this is impossible they can be cooked in a preheated 180°C, 375°F, Gas Mark 5 oven, for about 15-20 minutes.

1. Mix the softened butter with the parsley, sage, garlic, lemon rind and salt and pepper to taste.
2. Beat each escalope into a rectangle measuring about 20 cm (8 inches) × 13 cm (5 inches). Halve each escalope widthways; halve the slices of ham and cheese so that they are roughly the same size as the pieces of veal.
3. Spread each piece of veal with the flavoured butter. Top with a slice of ham, then with a slice of cheese.
4. Roll up each piece of veal tightly and neatly to enclose the ham and cheese; tie with string or coarse thread.
5. Put the veal rolls into a shallow dish, cover, and chill for 8 hours. [A]
6. To make the Aïoli, mix the garlic with the mustard, lemon juice, and salt and pepper to taste. Beat in the egg yolks and then whisk in the olive oil drop by drop. Finally stir in the Marsala. (The aïoli can be made in a food processor or liquidizer if preferred.) Put into a covered container and chill for 8 hours. [A]
7. Take 4 kebab skewers and thread 3 veal rolls lengthways on to each. Brush all over with the olive oil.
8. Cook on the greased grill of a preheated barbecue for 8-10 minutes, turning the skewers once. Remove the veal rolls from the skewers and cut off the strings.
9. Serve hot, garnished with sage leaves and lemon slices. Accompany with the Aïoli di Marsala and a fennel salad.
[A] The veal rolls and Aïoli can be made up to 24 hours in advance. Keep separate, cover and chill.

ITALY

COSTOLETTE FARCITE
Cheese-stuffed Veal Chops

4 thick lean veal chops
100 g (4 oz) Fontina or Bel Paese cheese, cut into 4 slices
2 tablespoons chopped fresh basil
1 large garlic clove, peeled and finely chopped
salt
freshly ground black pepper
2-4 tablespoons olive oil

Preparation time: 12-15 minutes
Cooking time: about 10 minutes

1. Cut through each veal chop horizontally from the nonbone side to form a deep pocket.
2. Press a slice of cheese well into the pocket of each chop. Mix the basil and garlic with salt and pepper to taste and sprinkle some inside each chop. [A]
3. Brush the stuffed chops on both sides with oil. Cook on the greased grill of a preheated barbecue (or under the grill) for 5 minutes on each side.
[A] Can be prepared up to 24 hours in advance.

CLOCKWISE FROM THE TOP Scaloppine al fontina e salvia;
Uccelletti di campagna senza testa; Costolette farcite

ITALY

UCCELLETTI DI CAMPAGNA SENZA TESTA
Pork, Ham and Sage Rolls

50 g (2 oz) sultanas
4 tablespoons Marsala
4 long thin pork escalopes, about 75 g (3 oz) each
4 thin slices Parma ham
1 tablespoon chopped fresh sage
salt
freshly ground black pepper
16 cubes white bread, about 2.5 cm (1 inch) square
4 tablespoons olive oil
8 thin rashers streaky bacon, rinded and halved crossways

Preparation time: 30 minutes, plus standing
Cooking time: 7-8 minutes

1. Mix the sultanas with the Marsala; cover and leave to stand for 1 hour.
2. Cut each pork escalope into 4 long strips; cut the slices of ham into strips roughly the same size.
3. Lay a strip of ham on top of each strip of pork. Sprinkle each strip with some chopped sage, a few of the plumped sultanas and salt and pepper to taste, then roll each strip up neatly, so that you have 16 sausage shapes.
4. Brush each cube of bread with olive oil, then roll in half a rasher of streaky bacon.
5. Thread 4 pork and ham rolls and 4 bread and bacon rolls alternately on to each of 4 kebab skewers; brush the skewers with olive oil.
6. Cook on the greased grill of a preheated barbecue (or under the grill) for 3-4 minutes on each side.
7. Serve hot with a vegetable dish such as Verdura Mista sulla Graticola (page 53).

FRANCE

GIGOT D'AGNEAU À LA CRÈME
Marinated Leg of Lamb with Cream Sauce

Serves 6-8
1 leg of lamb, weighing 2 kg (4¾ lb)
300 ml (½ pint) dry white wine
1 medium onion, peeled and thinly sliced
handful of celery leaves, roughly chopped
2 teaspoons juniper berries, crushed
salt
freshly ground black pepper
6 tablespoons olive oil
200 ml (⅓ pint) double cream

Preparation time: 15 minutes, plus chilling
Cooking time: 35-45 minutes for the first slices (see Mechoui page 28)

The lamb can be spit-roasted in the oven, but it will not have the lovely golden charred skin that it gets over the barbecue. Preheat the oven to 190°C, 375°F, Gas Mark 5, and remove cooked slices as and when they are ready.

1. With a small sharp knife, make several deep width-ways slits in the leg of lamb at regular intervals. Put the lamb into a shallow dish.
2. Mix the white wine with the onion, celery leaves, juniper berries and salt and pepper to taste: pour over the lamb.
3. Cover the lamb and chill for at least 6 hours, turning it from time to time. Ⓐ
4. Remove the lamb from its marinade and drain, reserving the marinade. Fix the joint securely on to the spit and brush all over with olive oil.
5. Spit-roast over the preheated barbecue for 35-45 minutes until the lamb is sufficiently tender to carve off the outer slices. If possible catch the meat juices as the joint cooks.
6. Whilst the lamb is cooking, make the sauce. Put the marinade into a pan and cook briskly until reduced by half. Stir in any meat juices and the cream; heat through gently and serve.
7. Keep the sauce warm on the side of the barbecue whilst the joint continues to cook. Carve off slices as they are ready.
Ⓐ Can be prepared in advance and left to marinate covered, for up to 24 hours.

FRANCE
OIE RÔTIE À LA BORDELAISE
Spit-roasted Goose

Serves 6
1 goose, weighing 4.5 kg (10 lb), plucked and drawn
salt
freshly ground black pepper
150 g (5 oz) button mushrooms, finely chopped
2 garlic cloves, peeled and crushed
14-15 anchovy fillets, finely chopped
225 g (8 oz) butter, softened
3 tablespoons chopped fresh parsley
1 goose liver, finely chopped (see below)

Preparation time: 25 minutes
Cooking time: 2-2½ hours

Although goose is a very fatty bird, the piquancy of the anchovy in the savoury butter offsets the natural richness of the meat. Ask your butcher for the giblets when you buy the goose, as the liver is used in the stuffing; if for any reason the goose liver has been discarded, use 2 or 3 chicken livers, chopped, instead. Like so many other whole birds, the goose does have a better flavour if it is cooked on a barbecue; if this is impossible, use an oven spit, cooking the goose at 190°C, 375°F, Gas Mark 5, for approximately the same length of time, keeping a deep drip tray under the bird.

1. Rub the goose inside and out with salt and pepper; prick the skin at regular intervals with a fine skewer.
2. Mix the mushrooms with the garlic, anchovy fillets, softened butter, parsley, goose liver and salt and pepper to taste.
3. Stuff the goose with the flavoured butter, then sew up the opening with fine string.
4. Fix the goose securely on the spit and roast over a preheated barbecue for 2 hours. Test to see if the bird is sufficiently cooked, if not, continue cooking for a further 20-30 minutes.
5. Carve the goose into fairly large slices. Serve with Cerises à l'aigre doux (page 58) and Crocchette di patate e vermicelli (page 55).

FRANCE
FILET DE BOEUF FLAMBÉ
Peppered Steak Flamed with Brandy

4 fillet steaks, about 175 g (6 oz) each
1 tablespoon finely crushed black peppercorns
salt
75 g (3 oz) butter, melted
2 cloves garlic, peeled and crushed
4 slices French bread, 1 cm (½ inch) thick, slightly larger
    than the steaks
4 tablespoons brandy

Preparation time: 8 minutes
Cooking time: 5-7 minutes (depending on how well you like your steak cooked)

1. Press both sides of each fillet steak into the crushed peppercorns and season with salt.
2. Heat the butter with the garlic. Brush the steaks on both sides with the garlic butter.
3. Place the steaks on a greased grill of a preheated barbecue and cook for about 2½-3½ minutes; turn the steaks over and cook for a further 2½-3½ minutes.
4. Just before the steaks are done to your liking, dip the French bread into the garlic butter, and toast quickly on both sides over the barbecue.
5. Place the toasted bread on a serving dish and arrange a cooked steak on each slice.
6. Pour the brandy into a heatproof ladle or small pan and heat over the barbecue; carefully set the brandy alight and pour it, flaming, over the steaks.
7. Serve as soon as the flames die down. Accompany with simple green salad.

To crush peppercorns (or other whole spices such as juniper berries or coriander) shape a piece of greaseproof paper into a cone, as for a piping bag (but do not cut off the end). Put the peppercorns inside and fold over the open end, making sure the corns are securely enclosed. Lay the cone on a chopping board and roll a rolling pin over the peppercorns until they have been crushed to the desired texture.

Oie rôtie à la bordelaise

FRANCE

POUSSINS FARCIS DE BOUCHERONS
Baby Chickens Stuffed with Goats' Cheese

4 poussins
salt
freshly ground black pepper
175 g (6 oz) soft goats' cheese e.g. Chèvre, Boucheron
1 tablespoon fresh thyme leaves
3 thin slices cured ham, finely chopped
1 lemon, cut into 8 wedges
Marinade:
200 ml (⅓ pint) olive oil
finely grated rind of 1 lemon
1 tablespoon chopped fresh basil

Preparation time: 35 minutes, plus chilling
Cooking time: 50-60 minutes
Oven: 180°C, 350°F, Gas Mark 4

The poussins can be cooked over the barbecue if preferred; cook them breast side down for 10 minutes, then turn the birds over and cook for another 15-20 minutes. Brush with the marinade from time to time during cooking, and test with a fine skewer to see that they are cooked through – they may take a little longer than stated, depending on their size.

1. Rub the poussins inside and out with salt and pepper.
2. Carefully slip your fingers between the skin and flesh of each poussin; starting at the neck end, gently ease the fingers along the length of the breastbone and down.
3. Mix the cheese with the thyme, ham and salt and pepper to taste.
4. Ease some of the cheese mixture evenly between the skin and flesh of each poussin. Stuff the body cavity of each poussin with 2 lemon wedges.
5. Mix the olive oil with the lemon rind, basil and salt and pepper to taste.
6. Put the poussins into a shallow dish; spoon the marinade over and cover with cling film. Chill for 4 hours. Ⓐ
7. Remove the poussins from their marinade and drain, reserving the marinade. Put them into a shallow oven-proof dish and cover with foil.
8. Cook in a preheated oven for 30 minutes, then remove the foil and brush with some of the marinade. Cook for a further 20-30 minutes.
9. Serve with a green salad.
Ⓐ The poussins can be prepared in advance and marinated for up to 24 hours.

Variation:
Instead of goat's cheese, use very smooth pâté in the stuffing.

FRANCE

LA PETITE SALADE DE CAILLE ET JAMBON
Quail, Artichoke and Smoked Ham Salad

8 quail, plucked and cleaned
salt
freshly ground black pepper
about 150 ml (¼ pint) walnut or olive oil
½ a medium head curly endive
8 canned artichoke hearts, well drained and quartered
4 thin slices Parma ham, cut into strips
100 g (4 oz) pâté de foie, chilled (see below)
1 garlic clove, peeled and crushed
1 tablespoon chopped fresh tarragon
3 tablespoons orange juice

Preparation time: 20-25 minutes
Cooking time: 20 minutes
Oven: 190°C, 375°F, Gas Mark 5

Real foie gras (goose liver) is exceedingly expensive and not essential for this dish. You can buy very good pâté de foie (smooth chicken liver pâté) from most supermarkets and good food shops for a fraction of the price. The quail can be cooked over the barbecue if preferred – wrap each bird in thin rashers of bacon and thread on to 1 or 2 large kebab skewers. Cook for 10-12 minutes.

1. Put the quail into a small roasting tin; season with salt and pepper and spoon 4 tablespoons of the walnut or olive oil over.
2. Cover with foil and cook in a preheated oven for 20 minutes – the quail should still be slightly pink.
3. Strip the leaves off the endive, discarding any that are wilted or discoloured; wash and shake dry. Arrange the leaves on a large, flat serving dish. Cut the pâté into 4 slices.
4. Arrange the artichoke quarters, strips of ham and slices of pâté around the edge of the dish.
5. Mix the remaining walnut oil with the garlic, tarragon, orange juice and salt and pepper to taste.
6. Halve the cooked quail using poultry shears or large kitchen scissors; discard any splintered pieces of bone. Arrange the quail halves, cut surface downwards, in the centre of the salad.
7. Spoon the prepared dressing over the quail and salad and serve immediately.

FROM THE LEFT La petite salade de caille et jambon; Cailles en brochette with Salade de pissenlits (page 46)

FRANCE

CAILLES EN BROCHETTE
Skewered Quails

8 quail, plucked and cleaned
finely grated rind of 1 orange
5 tablespoons olive oil
2 teaspoons crushed juniper berries
1 tablespoon chopped fresh rosemary
3 tablespoons brandy
salt
freshly ground black pepper
75 g (3 oz) coarse pâté e.g. Brêton, Pâté de Campagne
16 small thin rashers streaky bacon, rinded

Preparation time: 20 minutes, plus chilling
Cooking time: about 10 minutes

If you want to roast the quails, place them in a roasting dish (wrapped in their bacon), and cook in an oven preheated to 190°C, 375°F, Gas Mark 5 for about 20 minutes; if the quails are really tiny they may take slightly less time to cook.

1. Put the quail into a shallow dish. Mix the orange rind with the olive oil, crushed juniper berries, rosemary, brandy and salt and pepper to taste.
2. Spoon the marinade evenly over the quail; cover the dish and chill for 4-6 hours, turning the quails from time to time. Ⓐ
3. Remove the quails and drain, reserving the marinade. Press a generous knob of pâté into the centre of each quail, and wrap each bird in 2 rashers of bacon.
4. Thread the quails on to 2 large kebab skewers in such a way that the skewers hold the bacon in position.
5. Brush the quails with the marinade and cook on the greased grill of a preheated barbecue for 8-10 minutes until tender; turn them once during cooking. Serve with Salade de Pissenlits (page 46).
Ⓐ The quails can be marinated for up to 24 hours.

SALADS AND VEGETABLES

SALADE ANTIBOISE
Whiting, Eel, Potato and Beetroot Salad

300 ml (½ pint) dry white wine
3 tablespoons olive oil
1 small onion, peeled and sliced
1 tablespoon coarsely chopped fresh parsley
1 teaspoon crushed black peppercorns
salt
225 g (8 oz) conger eel, cleaned and cut into 2.5 cm (1 inch)
   sections
350 g (12 oz) whiting fillets
½ a cucumber, seeded and cubed
4 medium-size boiled potatoes, cubed
1 medium-size cooked beetroot, skinned and cubed
4 anchovy fillets, roughly chopped
1 teaspoon capers
8 tablespoons olive oil
2 tablespoons lemon juice
salt
freshly ground black pepper
1 tablespoon chopped fresh dill

Preparation time: 30 minutes, plus cooling
Cooking time: 30-35 minutes

This classic fish salad originates from the Antibes region, but it is enjoyed throughout the Côte d'Azur. The French often eat it with slices of crusty bread which have been dipped into garlicky olive oil.

1. Put the white wine into a pan with the olive oil, onion, parsley, peppercorns and salt to taste. Bring to the boil and simmer for 5 minutes.
2. Add the pieces of eel; cover the pan and simmer for 15 minutes.
3. Lay the whiting fillets on top of the eel; cover the pan and simmer gently for a further 10-15 minutes until the fish is just tender. Remove the fish and allow to cool.
4. Cut the whiting fillet into 5 cm (2 inch) pieces and put into a shallow bowl with the eel pieces, cucumber, potato, beetroot, anchovy fillets and capers.
5. Mix the oil with the lemon juice, salt and pepper to taste, and the chopped dill.
6. Stir the dressing into the other ingredients. Taste and adjust the seasoning.
7. Chill for at least 2 hours before serving. A
A Can be prepared in advance, covered, and kept chilled for a total of 8 hours.

SALAD NIÇOISE
Tomato, Tuna, Anchovy and Olive Salad

1 firm round lettuce
3 firm tomatoes (skinned if preferred), quartered
2 hard-boiled eggs, quartered
6 anchovy fillets, halved lengthways
12 black olives
2 teaspoons capers
1 × 200 g (7 oz) can tuna fish in oil, drained
1 medium red pepper, cored, seeded and cut into strips
6 tablespoons good quality green olive oil
1 large garlic clove, peeled and crushed
salt
freshly ground black pepper
1 tablespoon chopped fresh tarragon

Preparation time: 15-20 minutes

This is a very 'earthy' salad, and it should not look too arranged – although Salade Niçoise is colourful to look at and delicious to eat, it should almost look as if it has been 'thrown together'. I prefer to use just an oil based dressing, but you can add a little lemon juice or wine vinegar if preferred.

1. Keeping the lettuce whole, wash it well and shake dry. Remove the outer leaves and arrange them around the edge of a salad bowl; cut the remaining lettuce heart into quarters and place in the middle of the bowl.
2. Add the tomatoes, hard-boiled eggs, anchovy fillets, black olives, capers, tuna fish in chunks, and the strips of pepper.
3. Mix the oil with the garlic, salt and pepper to taste, and the chopped tarragon. Spoon the dressing evenly over the salad, and toss lightly before serving.

Salade Niçoise

FRANCE

TIAN DE TOMATES ET COURGETTES
Gratin of Rice and Tomatoes

at least 4 tablespoons olive oil
1 medium onion, peeled and finely chopped
225 g (8 oz) courgettes, diced
2 eggs
salt
freshly ground black pepper
50-75 g (2-3 oz) grated Parmesan cheese
4 tablespoons chopped fresh parsley
4 tablespoons cooked rice
2 tablespoons fresh white breadcrumbs
4 large tomatoes, halved and seeded

Preparation time: 20 minutes
Cooking time: about 25 minutes
Oven: 190°C, 375°F, Gas Mark 5

1. Heat half the olive oil in a pan and fry the onion gently for 3 minutes.
2. Add the courgettes and cook for a further 5 minutes.
3. Beat the eggs with salt and pepper to taste, and add the cheese, half the parsley and the cooked rice. Stir in the onion and courgette mixture.
4. Spread the vegetable and rice mixture evenly in a greased ovenproof gratin dish.
5. Mix the remaining chopped parsley with the breadcrumbs.
6. Push the halved tomatoes, cut sides uppermost, into the rice and vegetable mixture, easing them down until the tops are level with the mixture. Sprinkle the parsley and breadcrumbs over the tomatoes and drizzle the remaining olive oil evenly over the whole dish (you may need a little extra olive oil).
7. Bake in the oven for 15-17 minutes. Serve hot with barbecued fish such as Plaki Salonika (page 22). Ⓐ
Ⓐ Can be baked up to 24 hours in advance.

FRANCE

CHAMPIGNONS GRILLÉS À LA BOURGUIGNONNE
Mushrooms with Parsley and Garlic Butter

100 g (4 oz) unsalted butter, softened
2 large garlic cloves, peeled and crushed
1 teaspoon lemon juice
4 tablespoons finely chopped fresh parsley
salt
freshly ground black pepper
225 g (8 oz) even sized button mushrooms, wiped clean
2-3 tablespoons brandy

Preparation time: 20 minutes, plus chilling
Cooking time: 4-5 minutes

1. Mix the butter with the garlic, lemon juice, parsley, and salt and pepper to taste.
2. Divide the butter into 2 equal portions. F A Roll one of them into a short stubby sausage shape, wrap it in greaseproof paper and chill it thoroughly (or put it into the freezer for 1 hour).
3. Melt the other portion of flavoured butter. Put the mushrooms into a shallow flameproof dish and spoon the melted butter over.
4. Grill for 4-5 minutes until the mushrooms are tender.
5. Spoon the brandy over. Cut the chilled butter into slices and lay it on top of the mushrooms.
6. Serve immediately with French bread.
F Can be frozen (in 2 portions) for up to 1 month. Thaw until butter is soft enough to slice.
A Can be prepared up to 3 days in advance. Wrap the portions in greaseproof paper and keep chilled.

FRANCE

POIREAUX À LA PROVENÇAL
Leeks in Tomato, Olive and Lemon Sauce

750 g (1½ lb) leeks, halved, washed, and cut into 5 cm (2 inch) lengths
4 tablespoons olive oil
salt
freshly ground black pepper
grated rind of ½ lemon
4 large tomatoes, skinned, seeded and chopped
10 black olives, stoned and halved
3 tablespoons lemon juice

FRANCE

COURGETTES À LA GRECQUE
Courgettes in Herbed Oil

450 g (1 lb) courgettes, topped and tailed
1½ tablespoons salt
150 ml (¼ pint) olive oil
150 ml (¼ pint) water
1 bay leaf
1 tablespoon chopped fresh thyme
1 teaspoon coriander seeds, crushed
½ teaspoon black peppercorns, crushed
1 tablespoon lemon juice
4 large tomatoes, skinned, seeded and chopped
1 large garlic clove, peeled and finely chopped

Preparation time: 20 minutes, plus draining and chilling
Cooking time: 25-30 minutes

1. Cut each courgette into lengthways slices about ½ cm (¼ inch) thick.
2. Put the courgette slices into a colander and sprinkle with the salt; leave to drain for 1 hour. Rinse the courgette slices and pat them dry on paper towels.
3. Put the remaining ingredients into a deep frying pan. Bring to the boil and simmer for 5 minutes.
4. Add the courgette slices to the pan. Cover and simmer gently for about 20 minutes.
5. Transfer to a shallow serving dish; allow to cool and then chill for at least 2 hours. A
6. Serve as a starter with crusty bread, or as an accompaniment to barbecued fish.
A Can be prepared up to 24 hours in advance, covered and kept chilled until required.

Preparation time: 3 minutes
Cooking time: 22 minutes

1. Put the prepared leeks into a large shallow pan with the olive oil; add salt and pepper to taste, cover the pan, and simmer for 10 minutes.
2. Add the lemon rind, chopped tomatoes, halved olives and the lemon juice.
3. Simmer steadily, uncovered, for a further 10 minutes.
4. Serve hot as a vegetable, or chill and serve cold as a starter or salad.

CLOCKWISE FROM RIGHT Courgettes à la grecque;
Poireaux à la provençal; Champignons grillés à la bourguignonne

FRANCE

ARTICHAUTS AVEC MOUSSELINE DE CAVIARE
Globe Artichokes with Lumpfish Roe Mousseline

4 globe artichokes
½ a lemon
salt
2 tablespoons white wine vinegar
Dressing:
150 ml (¼ pint) olive oil
2 tablespoons lemon juice
freshly ground black pepper
1 garlic clove, peeled and crushed
Lumpfish roe mousseline:
150 ml (¼ pint) soured cream
1 teaspoon grated lemon rind
1 tablespoon finely chopped fresh parsley
75 g (3 oz) red lumpfish roe
To garnish:
2 tablespoons red lumpfish roe

Preparation time: 30 minutes, plus chilling
Cooking time: 30 minutes

Artichokes are abundantly available throughout the South of France. The small, pointed, underdeveloped artichokes are the same that are used for extracting the much prized *fonds d'artichaut* (artichoke hearts); whereas the larger, plumper artichokes are cooked to serve as a hot or cold starter with hollandaise sauce, hot melted butter or a vinaigrette dressing. The following recipe is a rather more interesting way of serving cooked artichokes; the centre leaves and choke are hollowed out, and the centre cavity is filled with a delicately flavoured mousseline filling – the base of each leaf is then dipped into the mousseline before eating.

1. With a sharp knife, cut off the top quarter to third of each artichoke. Snap off the stalks, break off any damaged outer leaves and trim the stalk ends neatly so that the artichokes will sit level. Rub all the cut surfaces with the lemon half to prevent discolouration. (It is not necessary to trim the points of the leaves, unless it is preferred for appearances sake.)
2. Rinse the artichokes well under cold running water to dislodge any grit between the leaves.
3. Bring a large pan of water to the boil and add a teaspoon of salt and the wine vinegar. Add the prepared artichokes, right way up, and cook steadily for about 30 minutes. Test the artichokes by removing a leaf from the base – if the fleshy base of the leaf is tender, then the artichoke is cooked.
4. Meanwhile make the dressing. Mix all the ingredients together, adding salt and pepper to taste.
5. Drain the cooked artichokes thoroughly, first in a colander, then upside down on paper towels.
6. Turn the artichokes the right way up. Twist and pull out the central cone of leaves in each one and reserve, exposing the hairy choke.
7. Scrape out the choke with a grapefruit spoon or teaspoon. Stand the artichokes upright on a dish and surround with the reserved centre leaves.
8. Spoon the prepared dressing over the artichokes and leaves. Cover and leave for 30 minutes.
9. Tip the artichokes so that any excess dressing drips off. Stand the artichokes upright on 4 individual serving dishes, surrounded by the reserved centre leaves.
10. Mix together all the lumpfish roe mousseline ingredients, adding salt and pepper to taste; Ⓐ spoon the mousseline into the centres of the artichokes.
11. Sprinkle each filled artichoke with a little lumpfish roe and serve with fingers of brown bread and butter.
Ⓐ The artichokes and mousseline can be prepared up to 6 hours in advance. Keep separate, cover and chill.

FRANCE

SALADE DE PISSENLITS
Dandelion Salad

450 g (¾ lb) dandelion leaves or mâche (see below)
2 tablespoons olive oil
75 g (3 oz) streaky bacon, rinded and chopped
2 tablespoons white wine vinegar
salt
freshly ground black pepper

Preparation time: 5 minutes
Cooking time: 3-4 minutes

Dandelion leaves and mâche can be bought in shops that specialize in French vegetables; or wild dandelion leaves can be used. If you cannot find either, use curly endive instead.

1. Wash the leaves, tear them into pieces and put in a bowl.
2. Heat the olive oil in a frying pan. Add the chopped bacon and fry gently until the bacon fat runs.
3. Add the wine vinegar and seasoning to taste and heat until the vinegar bubbles; spoon immediately over the dandelion leaves and toss well.
4. Serve immediately.

FROM THE LEFT Aïoli aigrossade; Artichauts avec mousseline de caviare

FRANCE

AÏOLI AIGROISSADE
Vegetables with Garlic Mayonnaise

Aïoli:
3 egg yolks
2 garlic cloves, peeled and crushed
2 tablespoons lemon juice
200 ml (⅓ pint) olive oil
salt
freshly ground black pepper
Vegetables:
175 g (6 oz) French beans, topped and tailed
225 g (8 oz) baby carrots, scraped or peeled
175 g (6 oz) tiny button mushrooms, stalks trimmed
175 g (6 oz) baby courgettes, stalks trimmed
225 g (8 oz) shelled broad beans
25 g (1 oz) butter (optional, see recipe)

Preparation time: 10-15 minutes
Cooking time: 6-8 minutes

The secret of this dish is the subtle combination of different temperatures and textures; the sauce should be cold and the vegetables hot, and the smoothness of the sauce should contrast with the slight crispiness of the lightly cooked vegetables. Vary the vegetables used according to seasonal availability.

1. To make the aïoli, whisk the egg yolks with the garlic and lemon juice. Whisk in the oil, drop by drop, as for a mayonnaise. Season to taste with salt and pepper. A
2. Wash the vegetables. Either lightly boil them separately in 5 small pans, or steam them, wrapping each variety in a small foil packet, putting a knob of butter inside. Remember that the vegetables should be slightly crunchy, so time the cooking carefully.
3. Drain the vegetables and arrange them on a warm serving dish; spoon the aïoli over the vegetables or serve in a small dish alongside. Serve immediately.
A Aïoli can be prepared in advance, covered, and kept chilled for up to 24 hours.

GREECE

HORIATIKI
Tomato and Feta Cheese Salad

350 g (12 oz) tomatoes, thinly sliced
1 medium onion, peeled and thinly sliced
2 teaspoons chopped fresh oregano or 1 teaspoon dried
   oregano
salt
freshly ground black pepper
100 g (4 oz) Feta cheese, crumbled
4-6 tablespoons olive oil

Preparation time: 10 minutes, plus standing

This is one of the simplest and yet most popular of the Greek salads; occasionally it contains other vegetable ingredients, but this combination has the 'cleanest' and freshest flavour. If prefered, finely shredded fennel can be used instead of tomatoes – the flavour and texture blends particularly well with Feta cheese.

1. Arrange the tomato and onion slices in a shallow serving dish.
2. Sprinkle with the oregano, salt and pepper to taste, and the crumbled Feta.
3. Spoon the olive oil evenly over the top and leave to stand at room temperature for 20 minutes to allow the flavours to mingle.
4. Serve the salad as a refreshing accompaniment to barbecued meats, such as kebabs.

GREECE

MELITZANO SALATA
Aubergine Purée

2 large aubergines, about 450 g (1 lb)
1 small onion, peeled and roughly chopped
2 garlic cloves, peeled and roughly chopped
4 tablespoons olive oil
2 tablespoons lemon juice
salt
freshly ground black pepper
To serve:
1-2 tablespoons chopped fresh parsley
black or green olives
pitta bread

Preparation time: 10 minutes
Cooking time: about 20 minutes

GREECE

TZATZIKI
Cucumber, Yogurt and Mint Salad

½ a large cucumber
salt
150 ml (¼ pint) plain unsweetened yogurt
1 tablespoon olive oil
1 garlic clove, peeled and crushed
2 tablespoons chopped fresh mint
freshly ground black pepper

Preparation time: 20-25 minutes, plus draining

Tzatziki is delicious as a sauce accompaniment to roast or barbecued lamb. It is also often served as part of a *meze* (a Greek mixed hors d'oeuvre).

1. Halve the cucumber lengthways and scoop out the seeds. (I always leave the cucumber peel on, but it can be removed if preferred.)
2. Chop the cucumber very finely and put it into a large sieve; sprinkle generously with salt (about 1½ tablespoons) and leave to drain over a bowl for 1 hour.
3. Rinse the cucumber pieces and pat dry on paper towels or a clean teatowel.
4. Mix the yogurt with the olive oil, garlic, mint, and salt and pepper to taste. Add the cucumber and stir well.
5. Serve immediately or cover and chill until required. Tzatziki is best eaten within 2-3 hours of making, otherwise it tends to turn rather watery.

This Greek dip has a much better flavour if the aubergines are scorched over the barbecue; if this is impossible bake them in a preheated 180°C, 350°F, Gas Mark 4 oven for 45-50 minutes.

1. Thread the aubergines on to a skewer. Place them on the greased grill of a preheated barbecue and cook for 10 minutes, then turn the aubergines over and cook for a further 10 minutes.
2. Leave the aubergines until they are sufficiently cool to handle, then peel them and chop the flesh on a wooden board.
3. Put the aubergine flesh into a liquidizer or food processor with the onion, garlic, olive oil, lemon juice and salt and pepper to taste; blend until smooth. (The purée can also be blended by hand.) Ⓐ
4. Transfer the purée to a bowl and sprinkle with the chopped parsley and garnish with the olives. Serve with pitta bread.
Ⓐ Can be prepared in advance and kept in the refrigerator for up to 36 hours if tightly covered.

GREECE

KOLOKYTHAKIA YIEMITSA
Stuffed Courgettes with Egg and Lemon Sauce

8 large plump courgettes
1 small onion, peeled and finely chopped
6 tablespoons olive oil
350 g (12 oz) finely minced lean lamb or beef
1 tablespoon chopped fresh oregano or 1 teaspoon dried
  oregano
2 tablespoons chopped fresh parsley
salt
freshly ground black pepper
4 tablespoons cooked rice
Egg and lemon sauce:
3 egg yolks
1 tablespoon water
6 tablespoons lemon juice
courgette juices (see recipe)

Preparation time: about 30 minutes
Cooking time: 45-50 minutes
Oven: 190°C, 375°F, Gas Mark 5

The egg and lemon sauce is the intricate part of this recipe; great care has to be taken otherwise the sauce is likely to curdle. The juices that come out of the courgettes during cooking are used as a base for the 'naturally thickened' sauce.

1. Top and tail each courgette. Using an apple corer or small sharp knife, 'tunnel through' each courgette, leaving an outer shell about 5 mm (¼ inch) thick.
2. Gently fry the onion in 2 tablespoons of the olive oil for 2 minutes. Add the minced meat and fry until lightly browned.
3. Mix the fried meat and onion with the oregano, parsley, salt and pepper to taste, and the cooked rice.
4. Pack each hollowed courgette tightly with the meat mixture. Arrange the stuffed courgettes in an oblong ovenproof dish and spoon the remaining oil over.
5. Bake the courgettes, uncovered, for 35-40 minutes, until tender.
6. Meanwhile start to prepare the sauce. Beat the egg yolks with the water, then beat in the lemon juice.
7. Once the courgettes are cooked, remove them carefully with a slotted spoon and place on a serving dish.
8. Whisk the egg yolk mixture into the hot cooking juices in the ovenproof dish. When the sauce thickens, spoon over the courgettes and serve.

CLOCKWISE FROM THE TOP Horiatiki; Tzatziki; Kolokythakia yiemitsa; Melitzano salata

GREECE

SPANAKOPITTA
Spinach and Phyllo Pie

Serves 6

1 kg (2½ lb) fresh spinach
1 large onion, peeled and thinly sliced
8 spring onions, chopped or thinly sliced
6 tablespoons olive oil
100 g (4 oz) butter, melted
salt
freshly ground black pepper
6 tablespoons chopped fresh parsley
4 tablespoons chopped fresh dill or oregano or 4 teaspoons
  dried
3 eggs, beaten
450 g (1 lb) phyllo pastry (see page 75)
1 tablespoon cold water

Preparation time: 30-35 minutes
Cooking time: 50-55 minutes
Oven: 190°C, 375°F, Gas Mark 5

1. Discard any wilted or discoloured spinach leaves and trim off all excess tough stalk from the remaining leaves. Wash the leaves and squeeze them dry. Shred.
2. Gently fry the onion and spring onions in 4 tablespoons of the olive oil and 25 g (1 oz) of the melted butter until soft but not brown.
3. Add the shredded spinach and stir over a moderate heat until evenly coated in fat. Cover and cook gently for 3-4 minutes.

4. Drain off any excess moisture from the spinach. Season with salt and pepper to taste, and mix in the parsley, dill or oregano and the beaten eggs.
5. Mix the remaining oil and melted butter together and lightly grease a rectangular tin or ovenproof dish, 35 × 25 × 7.5 cm deep (14 × 10 × 3 inches deep).
6. Brush a sheet of phyllo pastry with the melted butter and oil, and press it into the bottom and up the sides of the tin. Brush another sheet of phyllo pastry and place on top of the first one. Continue until you have put 7 layers of phyllo pastry, each brushed with butter and oil, into the tin.
7. Spread the spinach filling evenly over the layers of phyllo pastry; trim off the edges of the pastry with scissors, allowing a 2.5 cm (1 inch) overlap for shrinkage during cooking.
8. Lay another 7 layers of oiled phyllo pastry on top. Do not press the layers down, but trim off any unnecessary overlap as for the bottom layers.
9. Brush the top layer well with butter and oil. Using a sharp knife cut lengthways lines in the pastry and then cut across these to make squares or diamond shapes. Cut through only the top layers of pastry and not through to the spinach filling. F A
10. Sprinkle with 1 tablespoon of cold water.
11. Bake for 40 minutes until puffed and golden.
12. Let the spanakopitta stand for 5 minutes before cutting into portions.
F Can be frozen for up to 6 months. Thaw at room temperature for 3 hours before baking.
A Can be assembled up to 8 hours in advance, covered, and kept chilled until required.

GREECE

PATATES LATHERES ME LEMONI
Potato, Lemon and Thyme Casserole

Serves 4-6

1 kg (2 lb) potatoes, peeled
150 ml (¼ pint) olive oil
2 medium onions, peeled and sliced
2 tablespoons lemon juice
1 teaspoon grated lemon rind
150 ml (¼ pint) chicken stock
salt
freshly ground black pepper
1 tablespoon chopped fresh thyme

Preparation time: 10 minutes
Cooking time: about 40 minutes

1. Cut the potatoes into slices about 1 cm (½ inch) thick, and then halve each slice widthways. Wash the slices and pat them dry.
2. Heat the olive oil in a deep frying pan; add the sliced onions and cook until they start to colour.
3. Add the prepared potatoes and continue cooking over a moderate heat, stirring, until the onions and potatoes turn lightly golden.
4. Add the lemon juice, lemon rind, stock, salt and pepper to taste, and the thyme. Cover and cook slowly, stirring from time to time, for 25-30 minutes, by which time the water should have evaporated and the potatoes will be sitting in a richly flavoured oil.
5. Serve piping hot with a meat dish such as Souvlakia (page 33).

Spanakopitta

ALGERIA

TABBOULEH
Cracked Wheat and Mint Salad

Serves 4-6
225 g (8 oz) burghul (cracked wheat)
4 large spring onions, finely chopped
1 large garlic clove, peeled and crushed
4 tablespoons chopped fresh parsley
4 tablespoons finely chopped fresh mint
6 tablespoons olive oil
4 tablespoons lemon juice
salt
freshly ground black pepper
To serve:
black olives, prepared vine leaves, shredded lettuce etc.
  (see below)

Preparation time: 15 minutes, plus soaking and draining

There are many different ways of serving tabbouleh: in small bowls garnished with black olives; piled on to a layer of rinsed vine leaves; or heaped into a pyramid on a bed of shredded lettuce.

1. Put the burghul into a bowl and add sufficient water to cover; leave to stand for 45 minutes-1 hour. The burghul will swell up considerably.
2. Drain the burghul and squeeze out as much moisture as possible; drain the burghul more thoroughly by spreading it out on a clean teatowel.
3. Mix the drained burghul with the spring onions, garlic, parsley and mint.
4. Mix the olive oil with the lemon juice and salt and pepper to taste. Stir this dressing into the other ingredients.
5. Taste and adjust the seasoning – tabbouleh should be lemony and well-seasoned.
6. Serve as preferred, see suggestions above. Ⓐ
Ⓐ Can be prepared up to 24 hours in advance, covered and kept chilled until required.

CHACHOUKA
Pepper, Tomato and Egg Scramble

6 tablespoons olive oil
1 large onion, peeled and finely chopped
1 medium green pepper, cored, seeded and cut into strips
1 medium red pepper, cored, seeded and cut into strips
1 large garlic clove, peeled and crushed
450 g (1 lb) tomatoes, roughly chopped
6 eggs
salt
freshly ground black pepper
warm pitta bread, to serve

Preparation time: 15 minutes
Cooking time: about 25 minutes

This dish is traditionally scooped up from its serving dish with broken pieces of warm pitta bread.

1. Heat the olive oil in a medium size paella pan or large shallow frying pan and fry the onion and peppers gently for 10 minutes.
2. Add the garlic and tomatoes and cook fairly briskly for a further 8-10 minutes, stirring.
3. Beat the eggs with salt and pepper to taste; add to the pan and stir over the heat until the vegetable and egg mixture is creamy but still soft.
4. Serve immediately with warm pitta bread.

HUEVOS A LA FLAMENCA
Barbecued Eggs with Pepper and Sausage

1 large onion, peeled and thinly sliced
4 tablespoons olive oil
1 large garlic clove, peeled and crushed
225 g (8 oz) Chorizo sausage, thinly sliced
450 g (1 lb) tomatoes, skinned and chopped
1 large red pepper, cored, seeded and cut into strips
6 canned artichoke hearts, quartered
salt
freshly ground black pepper
75 g (3 oz) smoked ham, chopped
4 eggs

Preparation time: 15 minutes
Cooking time: 30 minutes

1. In a medium size paella pan or large shallow frying pan placed to one side on the barbecue grill, heat the olive oil and gently fry the onion.
2. Add the garlic and Chorizo sausage and fry gently for a further 3-4 minutes.
3. Add the tomatoes and red pepper and cook gently for about 15 minutes, stirring from time to time.
4. Add the artichoke hearts, salt and pepper to taste, and the smoked ham, and cook for a further 2-3 minutes.
5. Make 4 hollows in the mixture with the back of a spoon. Carefully crack one egg at a time into a cup and then slide it into a hollow.
6. Continue cooking over the barbecue until the eggs are just set and serve immediately.

FROM THE LEFT Chachouka; Huevos a la flamenca; Verdura mista sulla graticola

ITALY

VERDURA MISTA SULLA GRATICOLA
Mixed Barbecued Vegetables

Serves 6
2 large Spanish onions
2 green peppers
2 red peppers
2 large firm ripe tomatoes
1 large aubergine
salt
3 firm courgettes
12 large firm mushrooms
about 200 ml (⅓ pint) olive oil
coarsely ground black pepper
2 garlic cloves, peeled and crushed
2 tablespoons chopped fresh parsley

Preparation time: about 35-40 minutes
Cooking time: 25 minutes

1. Remove the brown outer skin from the onion, leaving the point intact. Cut in half horizontally.
2. Trim the stalk end of each pepper neatly.
3. Halve the tomatoes horizontally.
4. Cut the aubergine in half lengthways. Score the flesh, without cutting through the skin and sprinkle generously with salt. Leave to drain upside down on a wire tray for 30 minutes.
5. Cut the courgettes in half lengthways.
6. Trim the mushroom stalks.
7. Brush the cut surface of the onion with olive oil and place cut side down on the preheated barbecue.
8. Brush the peppers with olive oil and place on the barbecue grill; once the skin is charred, turn them so that another surface is in contact with the grill. Continue turning the peppers as each side becomes charred, eventually standing them upright.
9. Once they have cooled enough to handle, peel the peppers and cut them into strips, discarding the seeds. Put the strips into a bowl and add 4 tablespoons olive oil and salt and pepper. Stir in the garlic and the parsley.
10. Once the cut surfaces of the onions are charred, turn them over, making sure that they do not collapse, and move them to the edge of the barbecue grill.
11. Once the onions are charred all over and tender, cut them into chunks, discarding any parts that are very black. Add the onion to the peppers, stirring in a little extra oil.
12. Brush the cut surfaces of the tomatoes with oil and place cut side down on the grill. As soon as the flesh becomes slightly charred, turn them over.
13. Rinse the aubergine halves and pat them dry with paper towels. Brush the cut surfaces with oil and place cut side down on the barbecue grill; once the skin is dark brown, brush them with oil once again and turn them over. The aubergine is cooked when the centre flesh is creamy and tender. (It will become bitter if overcooked.)
14. When the tomatoes and aubergines are almost done, dip the courgette halves in oil and place them cut side down on the barbecue grill. Cook for 4-5 minutes.
15. Turn the courgettes over. Dip the whole mushrooms in oil and add to the grill. Cook for 3 minutes.
16. When the mushrooms, courgettes, tomatoes and aubergines are cooked, put them in a shallow serving dish, and serve with the cold onions and peppers.

MOROCCO

ASSIDA
Bean and Almond Soup

100 g (4 oz) dried white haricot beans
900 ml (1½ pints) chicken stock
100 g (4 oz) ground almonds
2 medium leeks, halved, cleaned and roughly chopped
2 garlic cloves, peeled and crushed
300 ml (½ pint) dry white wine
2 teaspoons caster sugar
salt
freshly ground black pepper
1 tablespoon chopped almonds, to garnish

Preparation time: 10 minutes, plus soaking and chilling
Cooking time: about 45 minutes

1. Soak the haricot beans in cold water for 8 hours or overnight.
2. Drain the beans. Put them into a pan with the chicken stock, bring to the boil and simmer steadily for 20 minutes.
3. Add the ground almonds, leeks, garlic, white wine, sugar, and salt and pepper to taste. Simmer gently, covered, for a further 25 minutes.
4. Sieve the soup, pushing through as much as possible, or blend it in a liquidizer until smooth. If the soup is too thick for your liking, add a little more stock.
5. Pour the soup into a large bowl. Cover and chill for 4-6 hours. F A
6. Serve the chilled soup in small bowls, sprinkled with the chopped almonds.
F Freeze for up to 6 months. Thaw in container in the refrigerator until just liquid.
A Can be prepared up to 24 hours in advance.

ITALY

CROCCHETTE DI PATATE E VERMICELLI
Crisp Potato and Vermicelli Croquettes

Serves 4-6
450 g (1 lb) potatoes, scrubbed
25 g (1 oz) butter
1 egg yolk
salt
freshly ground black pepper
large pinch of ground nutmeg
2 tablespoons grated Parmesan cheese
100 g (4 oz) vermicelli, coarsely crushed
3 tablespoons flour
vegetable oil, for deep frying

Preparation time: 30 minutes, plus chilling
Cooking time: about 26 minutes

1. Put the unpeeled potatoes into a pan with sufficient water to cover; bring to the boil and cook steadily until the potatoes are tender. Drain thoroughly and allow to cool slightly.
2. Peel the potatoes before they get too cold. Either mash them with a potato masher or put them into a liquidizer or food processor and blend until smooth.
3. Beat the butter, egg yolk, and salt and pepper and nutmeg to taste into the mashed potatoes. Mix in the Parmesan cheese.
4. Chill the potato mixture for 20 minutes so that it is easier to handle. Mix the crushed vermicelli with the flour.
5. Shape the potato mixture into small, plum-sized balls, and roll them in the flour and vermicelli mixture so that they are evenly coated. (If you find that the coating does not stick very well, dip the potato balls into beaten egg first.) F A
6. Deep fry the coated potato balls in hot oil for about 3 minutes on each side.
7. Drain thoroughly on paper towels and serve hot.
F Open-freeze the croquettes for about 1 hour. Pack into freezer bags. Allow to thaw at room temperature for 1 hour before deep frying.
A Can be prepared up to 8 hours in advance.

ITALY

CAVOLIFIORE FRITTO CON SALSA VERDE
Fried Cauliflower with Green Sauce

1 medium cauliflower
salt
squeeze of lemon juice
2 eggs
freshly ground black pepper
75 g (3 oz) fine dry breadcrumbs
vegetable oil, for shallow frying
Salsa verde:
6 anchovy fillets, finely chopped
3 tablespoons chopped fresh parsley
2 tablespoons capers, chopped
1 garlic clove, peeled and crushed
1 teaspoon mustard
1 tablespoon lemon juice
150 ml (¼ pint) olive oil
1 tablespoon white wine vinegar
freshly ground black pepper

Preparation time: 30 minutes, plus chilling
Cooking time: about 16 minutes

1. Trim the leaves and any excess stalk from the cauliflower; divide it into small even-sized florets.
2. Cook the florets in boiling salted water (to which you have added a squeeze of lemon juice) for about 8 minutes – the cauliflower should be just tender.
3. Drain the cauliflower thoroughly on paper towels.
4. Beat the eggs with black pepper to taste. Dip the florets first into the beaten egg and then into the breadcrumbs, making sure the florets are evenly coated. Chill for 1 hour. A
5. Meanwhile, make the sauce. Mix all the ingredients together very thoroughly in a liquidizer, food processor or by hand. A
6. Heat about 2 cm (¾ inch) of the vegetable oil in a deep frying pan. Lower the crumbed florets into the hot oil and fry over a moderate heat for 3-4 minutes on each side until golden.
7. Drain thoroughly on paper towels and serve piping hot with the Salsa Verde.
A The florets can be prepared up to 2 hours in advance. Salva Verde will keep for 4 days in a covered container in the refrigerator.

Variation:
Courgettes and aubergines, cut into 1 cm (½ inch) slices, can be prepared in the same way.

FROM THE LEFT Assida with Broa (page 70); Crocchette di patate e vermicelli; Cavolifiore fritto con salsa verde

FRESH AND SUN-DRIED FRUIT

FRANCE

FROMAGE BLANC AUX RAISINS SECS
Moulded Cream Cheese with Raisins

Serves 6-8
75 g (3 oz) raisins
3 tablespoons Calvados or Kirsch
450 g (1 lb) full fat soft cheese (unsalted)
2 tablespoons caster sugar
grated rind of ½ lemon
large pinch of ground cinnamon
4 egg whites
To serve:
150 ml (¼ pint) double or whipping cream (optional)
5-6 Figues au Four

Preparation time: 25 minutes, plus standing and chilling

This cream cheese dessert is traditionally made in a muslin-lined rush basket; you can use instead an empty tin (such as a ground coffee tin), piercing the bottom to make several holes, or a metal sieve 6 cm (2½ inches) in diameter. Alternatively, individual heart-shaped coeur à la crème moulds can be used.

1. Line the basket, container or moulds with a piece of clean muslin.
2. Mix the raisins with the Calvados or Kirsch and leave to stand for 30 minutes.
3. Beat the cheese with the sugar, lemon rind and cinnamon.
4. Whisk the egg whites until stiff but not dry, and fold lightly but thoroughly into the cheese mixture, together with the soaked raisins.
5. Turn the mixture into the muslin-lined container(s). Stand on a wire tray over a drip tray, cover and chill for 2 hours. [A]
6. Turn the moulded cheese(s) out on to a plate. Lightly whip the cream and spoon over the top. Serve with Figues au Four.
[A] Can be prepared up to 2 hours in advance, but must not be chilled for more than 4 hours in total.

Variation
Other dried fruits, such as chopped dried apricots, pears or pitted prunes can be used instead of raisins. For a really succulent result, use double the amount of Calvados or Kirsch, and leave the fruits to stand for a few hours or overnight.

FRANCE

FIGUES AU FOUR
Baked Figs in Wine

Serves 6
12 ripe firm fresh figs, stemmed
150 ml (¼ pint) medium dry white wine
2 tablespoons vanilla sugar
To serve:
double cream or Fromage blanc aux raisins secs

Preparation time: 8-10 minutes
Cooking time: about 15-20 minutes
Oven: 190°C, 375°F, Gas Mark 5

The figs can be cooked either in the oven or over the barbecue. If you are barbecueing them, there's no need to use a dish, simply wrap them completely in foil, and do not place them over the hottest part of the fire.

1. Cut a small cross in the stalk end of each fig.
2. Place the figs in a shallow ovenproof dish. Spoon the wine over and sprinkle with the vanilla sugar.
3. Cover with foil and cook in a preheated oven for about 15 minutes.
4. Serve warm, with cream or Fromage Blanc aux Raisins Secs.

> Vanilla sugar is made by enclosing a vanilla pod in a tightly closed storage jar full of caster sugar and leaving it for a couple of weeks. The sugar will absorb the vanilla flavour and can be used, with discretion, to flavour cakes, confectionery and milk drinks.

FROM THE TOP Figues au four; Fromage blanc aux raisins secs

FRANCE

GLACE À L'ABRICOT
Fresh Apricot Ice Cream

Serves 6
450 g (1 lb) fresh apricots, halved and stoned
150 ml (¼ pint) dry white wine
50 g (2 oz) caster sugar
Custard:
300 ml (½ pint) single cream
piece of vanilla pod, about 2.5 cm (1 inch) long
3 egg yolks
50 g (2 oz) caster sugar
150 ml (¼ pint) double or whipping cream

Preparation time: 45 minutes, plus cooling and freezing

Once you have tasted this delicious ice cream, you will never want to buy the commercial variety again; try a little Abricotine (apricot liqueur) poured over each portion.

1. Put the apricots into a pan with the white wine and sugar. Cover and cook gently until tender.
2. Meanwhile make the custard. Put the single cream and vanilla pod into a pan and bring just to the boil. Remove from the heat.
3. Lightly whisk the egg yolks with the sugar and gradually whisk in the strained scalded cream.
4. Transfer the mixture to the top of a double saucepan, or a bowl placed over a saucepan of water, and stir until the mixture is thick enough to coat the back of a wooden spoon. Allow to cool.
5. Beat the cooked apricots to a purée and combine with the custard.
6. Whip the cream until it is thick but not stiff. Fold lightly but thoroughly into the apricot custard with a metal spoon.
7. Put into ice trays or a shallow container and freeze for 1-2 hours, until the mixture has solidified at the edges.
8. Mash the ice cream with a fork, taking the outer ice cream into the centre of the tray.
9. Return the ice cream to the freezer for a further 2 hours. F Serve with Tortas de aceite (page 72).
F Can be frozen for up to 4 weeks. Overwrap the ice cream and remove from the freezer about 10-15 minutes before serving.

Variation
When fresh apricots are out of season, canned apricots can be used in their place. Choose a variety that has been canned in natural or apple juice and drain them well. Weigh the drained canned apricots; you will need approximately 450 g (1 lb). Liquidize the apricots to a purée (they do not require cooking), and proceed.

FRANCE

CERISES À L'AIGRE DOUX
Preserved Morello Cherries in Spiced Vinegar Syrup

450 g (1 lb) fresh morello cherries
350 ml (12 fl oz) white wine vinegar
175 g (6 oz) sugar
6 cloves

**Preparation time: 20 minutes, plus cooling
Cooking time: 10 minutes**

These sweet-sour cherries are usually eaten by the French as part of an hors d'oeuvre.

1. Make sure that none of the cherries are bruised or damaged, then wipe them clean with a damp cloth.
2. Trim the stalks to about 2.5 cm (1 inch) long.
3. Pack the cherries into a clean preserving jar; the jar should be about three-quarters full of fruit.
4. Put the vinegar into a pan with the sugar and cloves. Bring to the boil and simmer steadily for 10 minutes.
5. Allow the vinegar syrup to cool completely and then pour over the cherries.
6. Fasten the jar. Leave for 3 weeks before opening.

FROM THE LEFT Glace à l'abricot; Pêches aux fraises

FRANCE

PÊCHES AUX FRAISES
Peaches with Strawberry Purée

Serves 6
6 ripe peaches
300 ml (½ pint) sweet white wine
2 teaspoons powdered gelatine
12 tablespoons orange juice
225 g (8 oz) strawberries, hulled
2 tablespoons caster sugar

Preparation time: 35 minutes, plus marinating and chilling

This is just one of the many delicious fresh fruit desserts which are made in the Mediterranean countries. The peaches found in the French markets are much cheaper than those that we buy in this country; nevertheless, it is a dessert that is well worth trying.

1. Score a cross in the skin at the stalk end of each peach. Plunge them into boiling water for 30 seconds and then slip off the skins.
2. Put the skinned peaches into a dish and pour the white wine over. Cover and marinate in a cool place for 4 hours.
3. Remove the peaches from their white wine marinade and drain. Put the marinade into a bowl.
4. Dissolve the gelatine in 6 tablespoons of the orange juice and stir into the marinade. Leave to thicken.
5. Blend the strawberries in a liquidizer or food processor with the remaining orange juice and sugar to make a smooth purée.
6. Pour the strawberry purée into a glass serving dish and place the whole peaches on top.
7. As soon as the white wine glaze is syrupy, spoon it over the peaches. Ⓐ Chill for 1 hour before serving. Ⓐ Can be prepared up to 6 hours in advance.

Variation:
When peaches are out of season, canned whole peaches can be used instead. Canned or defrosted frozen strawberries can be used in place of fresh ones, but you will need to adjust the consistency of the purée accordingly.

ITALY

SOUFFLÉ DI AMARETTO
Peach and Almond Soufflé

Serves 6
6 eggs, separated
100 g (4 oz) caster sugar
3 tablespoons Amaretto liqueur
300 ml (½ pint) peach purée (see below)
20 g (¾ oz) powdered gelatine
3 tablespoons sweet white wine
300 ml (½ pint) double or whipping cream
To decorate:
3 tablespoons flaked almonds, lightly toasted
2 tablespoons icing sugar

Preparation time: 30 minutes, plus chilling

The peach purée gives the soufflé a much better flavour if it is made from skinned and stoned fresh peaches, but you can use drained canned peaches as a substitute. (You may need to add a little extra sugar to fresh peaches.) The soufflé is absolutely delicious if it is frozen and then served semi-frozen, rather like ice cream.

1. Put the egg yolks into a bowl with the caster sugar and Amaretto liqueur. Whisk until thick, light and creamy.
2. Whisk in the peach purée.
3. Put the gelatine and wine into a small bowl. Stand the bowl in a pan of hot water and stir until the gelatine has dissolved.
4. Whisk the dissolved gelatine into the peach mixture.
5. Fix a deep collar of lightly greased, doubled, greaseproof paper around the edge of a lightly greased 900 ml (1½ pint) soufflé dish.
6. Lightly whip the cream and fold gently but thoroughly into the peach mixture. Whisk the egg whites until thick and fold in.
7. Pour into the prepared soufflé dish. Chill until set (about 4 hours). F A
8. Sprinkle with the toasted almonds and dust with icing sugar.
F Freeze for up to 1 month. Thaw for 20 minutes at room temperature and serve semi-frozen, or allow it to thaw completely for about 1 hour at room temperature.
A Can be prepared up to 24 hours in advance, covered, and kept chilled.

Variation:
Many fresh fruits blend well with the flavour of Amaretto liqueur. Instead of using fresh peach purée, you can use a purée of skinned, stoned apricots, mangoes or nectarines.

ITALY

MACEDONIA DI FRUTTA AL STREGA
Mixed Fresh Fruit in Strega Syrup

300 ml (½ pint) dry white wine
75 g (3 oz) sugar
grated rind of ½ lemon
4 tablespoons Strega liqueur
2 large ripe peaches
6 ripe apricots
4 large ripe plums
8 small fresh purple figs
Ricotta cream:
100 g (4 oz) ricotta or cottage cheese
4 tablespoons double or whipping cream
2 tablespoons Strega liqueur

Preparation time: 30 minutes, plus cooling and chilling
Cooking time: 2 minutes

Strega is one of the most popular of the Italian liqueurs; it is made from a delicate blending of different herbs, and has a distinct vanilla flavour. Its deep golden colour lends a rich glow to fresh fruit salads.

1. Put the wine into a pan with the sugar and lemon rind. Stir over gentle heat until the sugar has dissolved.
2. Allow the syrup to cool, then stir in the Strega.
3. Cut a small cross in the stalk ends of the peaches and apricots; scald in boiling water for 30 seconds and slip off the skins.
4. Cut the peaches around the middle and twist to separate the 2 halves; discard the stones and cut the peach halves into slices.
5. Cut the apricots and plums around the middle and twist to separate the 2 halves, discarding the stones.
6. The figs can either be left whole, or cut in half lengthways.
7. Add the prepared fruits to the Strega syrup, stirring them until evenly coated. Chill, covered, for 1 hour.
8. For the Ricotta cream, sieve the cheese and beat in the cream and the Strega. Cover and chill for 1 hour.
9. Serve the Macedonia di Frutta accompanied with the Ricotta cream.

CLOCKWISE FROM THE LEFT Macedonia di frutta al Strega;
Soufflé di Amaretto; Ciliege al Marsala

ITALY

CILIEGE AL MARSALA
Cherries in Marsala

300 ml (½ pint) Marsala
2 strips orange peel
75 g (3 oz) sugar
350 g (12 oz) blackish-red cherries, stoned
fine strips of orange peel, to decorate

Preparation time: 20 minutes, plus chilling
Cooking time: 20 minutes

The cherries are best eaten chilled, but can be served hot if preferred.

1. Put the Marsala, orange peel and sugar into a pan and stir over a gentle heat until the sugar has dissolved.
2. Simmer the Marsala syrup for 5 minutes.
3. Add the prepared cherries to the syrup. Cover the pan and simmer gently for about 10 minutes.
4. Allow the cherries to cool in their syrup, cover and chill for 3-4 hours. **A**
5. Serve the cherries in small dishes, topped with fine strips of orange peel. Serve with whipped cream.
A Can be prepared up to 8 hours in advance.

GREECE

YAOURTI ME KYTHANIA
Sweetened Yogurt with Quince

450 g (1 lb) quinces or under-ripe nectarines
100 g (4 oz) sugar
200 ml (⅓ pint) water
4 tablespoons lemon juice
300 ml (½ pint) thick plain unsweetened yogurt
    (preferably Greek)
2 tablespoons honey
grated rind of ½ lemon

Preparation time: 20 minutes, plus chilling
Cooking time: about 35 minutes

Greek yogurt can be bought in this country, and it has quite a different texture from most other natural yogurts – it is well worth trying.

1. Peel and core the quinces or nectarines and cut into thick slices, reserving the peel.
2. Put the sugar, water and lemon juice into a pan and stir over a gentle heat until the sugar has dissolved.
3. Put the reserved peel into the pan and simmer gently for about 20 minutes until thick and syrupy.
4. Strain the syrup and return to a clean pan.
5. Add the fruit slices and poach gently until tender – about 15 minutes.
6. Allow the fruit slices to cool in the syrup and then chill.
7. Mix the yogurt with the honey and lemon rind.
8. Spoon the fruit slices and syrup into small dishes and top with the flavoured yogurt.

MOROCCO

TMAR MIHCHI
Pistachio-filled Candied Dates

Makes about 48
225 g (8 oz) unsalted pistachio nuts, shelled
850 g (1 lb 14 oz) sugar
6 teaspoons rosewater (see page 28)
48 plump dates, stoned
450 ml (¾ pint) water
large pinch of cream of tartar
225 g (8 oz) lump sugar, coarsely crushed
1 teaspoon ground cinnamon

Preparation time: 35-40 minutes, plus standing for 1 day
Cooking time: 15-20 minutes
Oven: 190°C, 375°F, Gas Mark 5

1. Scald the pistachio nuts in boiling water for 1 minute. Remove the nuts with a draining spoon and slip off the skins.
2. Toast the skinned nuts in the oven for 5 minutes, until lightly golden.
3. Put the pistachios into a liquidizer or food processor with 175 g (6 oz) of the sugar and grind quite finely.
4. Add the rosewater to the nut mixture and blend to a smooth paste.
5. Open up each date along the side it has been stoned.

Press a small spoonful of the pistachio paste into each date and pinch the opening together.
6. Put the water into a heavy-based pan with the remaining granulated sugar and the cream of tartar. Stir over a gentle heat until the sugar has dissolved.
7. Boil the syrup until it reaches a temperature of 107°C (225°F) on a sugar thermometer, or until a little dropped into a cup of cold water forms a fine thread.
8. Remove the pan from the heat immediately.
9. Mix the crushed sugar with the ground cinnamon and place in a shallow dish.
10. Spike each date on to a skewer. Dip it into the syrup until evenly coated, allow the excess to drip off, then roll the date in the spiced sugar. Slide off on to greaseproof paper.
11. Pack the dates in single layers, between greaseproof paper. Keep at room temperature for 1 day before serving with black coffee. Will keep for 1 week in a cool place.

 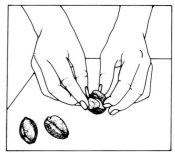

Removing the stone   Pressing in the filling

ITALY

FRULLATI DI FRUTTA
Fresh Fruit Shake

Serves 2
1 banana
1 ripe peach, peeled
6 medium-size ripe strawberries, washed
150 ml (¼ pint) milk
2 teaspoons vanilla sugar (page 56)
3 tablespoons crushed ice
½ teaspoon ground cinnamon

Preparation time: 5 minutes

A frullati is very similar to a milkshake, but it has a fresher flavour. They are often served in Italian cafes, as a between-meal drink, and children love them. If you are preparing a frullati for an adult, add a little liqueur such as Strega or Maraschino when you blend it. Other fruits can be used instead of banana and peach – for example apricots and raspberries.

1. Peel and chop the banana. Halve the peach, removing the stone, and chop the flesh. Hull the strawberries.
2. Put the banana, peach and strawberries into a liquidizer with the milk, vanilla sugar, crushed ice and cinnamon.
3. Blend until the ice has dissolved completely.
4. Sweeten to taste and serve immediately.

LEFT Tmar mihchi

SPAIN

SOPA HELADA
Iced Melon Soup

1 small ripe honeydew melon, chilled
50 g (2 oz) fine fresh white breadcrumbs
50 g (2 oz) ground almonds
2 garlic cloves, peeled and crushed
150 ml (¼ pint) olive oil
150 ml (¼ pint) dry white wine, chilled
8 ice cubes

Preparation time: 20-25 minutes

Gazpacho, the Spanish cold vegetable soup, was always my favourite summer soup, until I discovered this wonderfully refreshing soup based on melon. It is a perfect soup to serve in hot weather; do make a good quantity as people are bound to come back for seconds. It has a rather unusual, granular texture, I find it unnecessary to season the soup, but this is very much a matter of personal preference.

1. Halve and seed the melon. Remove the peel and cut the flesh into 1 cm (½ inch) cubes.
2. Mix the breadcrumbs with the ground almonds, garlic, olive oil and wine.
3. Stir in the melon cubes and the ice cubes.
4. As soon as the ice starts to melt, ladle the soup into small glass bowls.

Of the Mediterranean countries, Greece, France, Italy and Spain all produce their own olive oil, which is used extensively in their national dishes, giving them a distinct and delicious flavour. Olive oils can vary enormously in colour and flavour; some, like those from Provence in Southern France, are pale and delicate, while others, like the green olive oil from Greece, are heavy and fruity. The finest olive oil (often referred to as 'cold pressed' or 'extra vergine') is pressed cold from fresh ripe fruits and is a pale clear yellowish green, odourless and delicately flavoured. It's always worth investing in the best olive oil you can buy.

SPAIN

NARANJAS AL VINHO VERDE
Fruits Steeped in White Wine

4 oranges
175 g (6 oz) black cherries, stoned
175 g (6 oz) green grapes, pips removed
3 tablespoons caster sugar
50 g (2 oz) flaked almonds
mixed spice, for sprinkling
300 ml (½ pint) Vinho Verde or other dry crisp white wine such as Aligoté

Preparation time: 30 minutes, plus chilling

1. Remove all the peel and pith from the oranges. Cut each one into thin slices.
2. Arrange the orange slices, black cherries and grapes in layers in a glass dish, sprinkling each layer with a little sugar, a spoonful or two of almonds and a sprinkling of mixed spice.
3. Pour the wine over.
4. Cover and chill well for 4 hours. 🅰
🅰 Can be prepared up to 24 hours in advance, covered and kept chilled until required.

FROM THE LEFT Naranjas al Vinho Verde; Crema al jerez; Sangria

SPAIN

CREMA AL JEREZ
Sherried Cream with Figs, Dates and Walnuts

6 small ripe figs, stemmed and quartered (see below)
100 g (4 oz) stoned dates
6 tablespoons cream sherry
75 g (3 oz) walnuts, coarsely chopped
150 ml (¼ pint) double or whipping cream

Preparation time: 20 minutes, plus marinating

Fresh figs are traditionally used in this recipe, but you can use the dried variety if fresh ones are unavailable; plump dried figs beforehand by soaking them in warm wine or water for about 2 hours.

1. Put the figs and dates into a bowl with 4 tablespoons of the sherry.
2. Cover and leave to marinate for about 1-4 hours. (This can be done at room temperature.)
3. Stir the chopped walnuts into the fruits.
4. Whip the cream, adding the remaining sherry.
5. Spoon the steeped fruits and nuts into stemmed glasses or bowls and top with the sherried cream.

SPAIN

SANGRIA
Wine and Fruit Cup

1 lemon, thinly sliced
1 thin-skinned orange, thinly sliced
1 eating apple, halved, cored and cut into wedges
50 g (2 oz) caster sugar
1 × 75 cl bottle red Rioja wine
4 tablespoons brandy
1 large sprig of mint
300 ml (½ pint) soda water, chilled

Preparation time: 10 minutes, plus chilling

1. Put the prepared lemon, orange and apple into a tall jug.
2. Sprinkle the sugar over and add the red wine, brandy and mint.
3. Cover and chill for 1 hour Ⓐ.
4. Press down well on the fruit with a wooden spoon and stir in the chilled soda water.
5. Pour into well chilled wine glasses or glass mugs, adding a little of the fruit to each one.
Ⓐ Can be prepared up to 4 hours in advance.

BUNUELOS DE PLATANO
Spanish Banana Fritters

4 firm ripe bananas
4 tablespoons lemon juice
4 tablespoons Spanish brandy
Batter:
50 g (2 oz) plain flour
pinch of salt
1 egg, beaten
1 tablespoon melted butter
6 tablespoons milk
1 egg white
flour, for dusting
oil, for deep frying
3 tablespoons icing sugar, for dusting

Preparation time: 25 minutes, plus standing
Cooking time: 3-4 minutes

1. Peel the bananas and halve them crossways.
2. Put the bananas into a shallow dish with the lemon juice and brandy. Stir the bananas in the brandy liquid and put to one side for 20 minutes.
3. Meanwhile prepare the batter: sift the flour and salt into a large mixing bowl. Beat in the beaten egg, melted butter and milk and mix until the batter is quite smooth.
4. Whisk the egg white until fairly stiff and fold lightly into the batter.
5. Drain the banana pieces on paper towels.
6. Dust the banana pieces with flour, then dip each one into the prepared batter. Heat the oil in a deep frying pan to 180°-190°C/350°-375°F or until a cube of bread browns in 30 seconds. Lower the banana pieces into the pan and deep fry for about 3-4 minutes until crisp and golden.
7. Drain the banana fritters thoroughly on paper towels.
8. Dust immediately with a generous dredging of icing sugar, and serve piping hot.

Variation:
Many other fruits can be used for making fritters, such as thick rings of cored apple, halved and stoned fresh apricots, halved and stoned fresh plums, or halved and stoned fresh peaches. Adjust the frying times slightly according to the texture and size of the pieces of fruit.

FLAN DE NARANJA
Orange Caramel Custard

Serves 6-8
Caramel:
225 g (8 oz) sugar
4 tablespoons water
Custard:
2 oranges
900 ml (1½ pints) milk
1 large cinnamon stick
piece of vanilla pod, about 5 cm (2 inches) long
6 eggs
2 egg yolks
225 g (8 oz) caster sugar

Preparation time: 30 minutes, plus chilling
Cooking time: about 50 minutes
Oven: 160°C, 325°F, Gas Mark 3

1. To make the caramel, put the sugar and water in a heavy-based pan. Stir over a gentle heat until the sugar has dissolved.
2. Bring to the boil and cook briskly, without stirring, until the syrup darkens to a deep golden caramel.
3. Quickly swirl the caramel around the sides and base of greased individual deep dariole moulds or ovenproof dishes.
4. Thinly pare the rind from the oranges; remove all the pith and divide the flesh into segments, cutting between the membranes.
5. Put the milk into a pan with the orange rind, cinnamon stick and vanilla pod; bring to just below boiling point. Strain.
6. Meanwhile whisk the eggs with the egg yolks and sugar until thick, light and creamy.
7. Gradually whisk in the strained, flavoured milk.
8. Place a few orange segments in each caramel-lined mould and top with strained custard.
9. Stand the moulds in a roasting tin and add sufficient hot water to come halfway up the sides of the moulds. Bake in a preheated oven for about 35 minutes until set.
10. Remove the custards from the roasting tin and allow to cool. Chill for 2 hours. Ⓐ
11. Dip the base of each mould into a bowl of warm water, and then carefully turn each custard upside down on to a serving plate.
Ⓐ Can be prepared up to 24 hours in advance.

FROM THE TOP Bunuelos de platano; Flan de naranja

SPAIN

DULCE DE MEMBRILLO
Quince Cheese

Serves 4-6
750 g (1½ lb) ripe quinces
about 450 g (1 lb) sugar (see recipe)
2 tablespoons lemon juice

Preparation time: 15 minutes, plus chilling
Cooking time: 35-40 minutes

Dulce de Membrillo is usually bought in cans; it is thick enough to be turned out and cut into slices, and is usually eaten with cheese – traditionally with Spanish Manchego cheese, or with any other cheese that has a fairly bland flavour and soft texture, such as curd cheese.

1. Wipe the outer skins of the quinces and cut them into small pieces – there is no need to peel or core them.
2. Put the quinces into a pan and add sufficient water *barely to cover.*
3. Simmer for about 20 minutes until the fruit is quite soft. Remove the stones.
4. Push the cooked quinces through a sieve and weigh the fruit purée.
5. Put the purée into a clean pan and to every 450 g (1 lb) of purée add 450 g (1 lb) sugar. Stir in the lemon juice.
6. Boil gently until the quince mixture is thick and will set when a little is spooned on to a cold saucer.
7. Pour the mixture into a lightly greased shallow dish and chill until set. Ⓐ
8. Turn the quince cheese out on to a serving dish. Cut into slices and serve with cheese (see above).
Ⓐ Can be made up to 48 hours in advance.

PASTRIES AND PUDDINGS

ITALY

CASSATA ALLA SICILIANA
Ricotta and Candied Fruit Cake

Serves 6
350 g (12 oz) ricotta or cottage cheese
100 g (4 oz) caster sugar
25 g (1 oz) vanilla sugar (page 56)
150 ml (¼ pint) double or whipping cream
175 g (6 oz) crystallized fruits, chopped, or chopped mixed
    peel
25 g (1 oz) shelled pistachio nuts, chopped
3 plain sponge layers, each 18 cm (7 inches) in
    diameter × 2 cm (¾ inch) deep
4 tablespoons Strega
Icing:
175 g (6 oz) butter, softened
275 g (10 oz) icing sugar, sifted
100 g (4 oz) plain chocolate, melted
3 tablespoons cold strong black coffee
1 tablespoon chocolate coffee beans

Preparation time: 50 minutes, plus chilling overnight

1. Sieve the cheese and beat in the caster sugar and vanilla sugar.
2. Whip the cream and beat it into the cheese mixture, then stir in the chopped fruit or peel and nuts.
3. Sprinkle each sponge layer with the Strega. Put one sponge layer into the bottom of a deep 18 cm (7 inch) cake tin.
4. Cover the sponge layer with half the cheese and fruit mixture, then insert a second sponge layer on top.
5. Cover the second sponge layer with the remaining cheese and fruit mixture, and top with the remaining sponge layer.
6. Lay a plate on top and lay a 450 kg (1 lb) weight on top of that. Chill overnight. A
7. To make the icing, beat the butter with the icing sugar, melted chocolate and black coffee. Chill for 2 hours. A
8. Turn the chilled cake out on to a serving plate.
9. Swirl the icing evenly over the top and sides. Decorate with the chocolate coffee beans. F
A The chilled cake can be assembled and the icing made up to 1 day in advance; keep separate, cover and chill.
F Thaw at room temperature for 3 hours.

ITALY

DOLCE DI RISO E LIMONE
Iced Lemon Rice Pudding

Serves 4-6
thinly pared rind of 1 lemon
600 ml (1 pint) milk
50 g (2 oz) caster sugar
100 g (4 oz) Italian round-grain or pudding rice
finely grated rind of 1 lemon
2 eggs
To serve:
thinly pared lemon rind
4-6 Amaretti biscuits

Preparation time: 15-20 minutes, plus standing and chilling
Cooking time: 27 minutes

1. Put the pared lemon rind into a pan with the milk; bring just to the boil and leave to infuse for 30 minutes.
2. Strain the milk into a clean pan and stir in the sugar.
3. Stir in the rice and cook gently until the rice is tender but still slightly firm and all the milk has been absorbed, about 25 minutes.
4. Turn the rice into a bowl and beat in the grated lemon rind and the eggs.
5. Turn into a greased 900 ml (1½ pint) mould. Chill for 4-6 hours. A
6. Carefully turn out the set rice on to a serving dish. Decorate with strips of lemon rind and serve with Amaretti biscuits (small Italian macaroons).
A Can be prepared up to 24 hours in advance.

SPAIN

BROA
Fine Corn Bread

Makes 1 round loaf
250 g (9 oz) fine yellow cornmeal or semolina (see below)
1 teaspoon salt
1 teaspoon caster sugar
250 ml (8 fl oz) boiling water
1 tablespoon olive oil
3 tablespoons tepid water
15 g (½ oz) fresh yeast or 2 teaspoons dried yeast
about 200 g (7 oz) plain flour, sifted
Topping: (optional)
2-3 tablespoons milk
1 tablespoon poppy seeds

Preparation time: 35-40 minutes, plus standing and rising
Cooking time: 40-45 minutes
Oven: 190°C, 375°F, Gas Mark 5

You need a fine yellow cornmeal or semolina for broa; if you can only find one that is medium ground put it into the liquidizer and grind to a finer texture.

1. Put 175 g (6 oz) of the cornmeal into a large mixing bowl with the salt, sugar, boiling water and olive oil; beat until smooth. Put on one side while you prepare the yeast.
2. Put the tepid water into a cup or small bowl and crumble in the yeast. Leave in a warm place to froth – about 10 minutes.
3. Stir the yeast liquid into the cornmeal and sugar mixture, gradually adding the remaining cornmeal and 100 g (4 oz) of the flour. Work to a smooth dough.
4. Shape the dough into a ball. Place in a large mixing bowl, dust lightly with flour, cover with a clean, damp teatowel and leave in a warm, draught-free place, until the dough has doubled in bulk – about 30 minutes.
5. Grease the base and sides of a 23 cm (9 inch) loose-bottomed, deep-sided, fluted flan tin.
6. Turn the dough out on to a lightly floured work surface, and knead for about 5 minutes with a forwards and backwards motion, working in an extra 50-75 g (2-3 oz) of plain flour, to give a firm but not stiff dough.
7. Shape the dough into a round loaf and place in the prepared tin.
8. Cover with a clean, damp teatowel and leave to rise in a warm place for 30 minutes or until doubled in bulk.
9. If liked, brush the top of the dough with the milk and sprinkle with the poppy seeds.
10. Bake in a preheated oven for 40-45 minutes until golden, risen and cooked through.
11. Transfer the bread to a wire tray and allow to cool slightly. F Serve warm. This is a traditional accompaniment to both hot and cold soups.
F Thaw at room temperature for 1 hour, then warm through in a moderate oven, or reheat from frozen at 150°C, 300°F, Gas Mark 2.

SPAIN

TORRIJAS
Sweet Fried Bread Fingers

Makes 18
100 g (4 oz) plain chocolate, broken into small pieces
250 ml (8 fl oz) milk
1 egg yolk
6 thick slices white bread, crusts removed
oil for shallow frying
50 g (2 oz) caster sugar
To decorate:
200 ml (⅓ pint) double or whipping cream
3 tablespoons redcurrant jelly, sieved

Preparation time: 25-30 minutes
Cooking time: 6-8 minutes

1. Put the chocolate into a saucepan with the milk; stir over a gentle heat until the chocolate has dissolved.
2. Allow to cool slightly, then beat in the egg yolk.
3. Cut each slice of bread into 3 fingers.
4. Heat about 1 cm (½ inch) depth of oil to 180°-190°C/350°-375°F, or until a cube of bread browns in 30 seconds, in a large shallow pan. Dip the bread fingers into the chocolate milk, allowing excess milk to drain off.
5. Lower the bread fingers into the hot oil and fry gently for 2-3 minutes on each side.
6. Drain the fingers thoroughly on paper towels, dust with the caster sugar and allow to cool.
7. Whip the cream and pipe a line along the centre of each bread finger.
8. Pipe a spiral of redcurrant jelly on top of the cream. A
A Can be prepared up to 1 day in advance. Store in an airtight tin, layered with greaseproof paper.

FROM THE TOP Pandolce; Broa

ITALY

PANDOLCE
Crystallized Fruit and Nut Bread

Serves 8

20 g (¾ oz) fresh yeast or 3 teaspoons dried yeast

100 g (4 oz) caster sugar

4 tablespoons tepid water

450 g (1 lb) plain flour

75 g (3 oz) butter, melted

1 egg, beaten

225 g (8 oz) crystallized fruits, chopped or chopped mixed
   peel

75 g (3 oz) blanched almonds, chopped

**Preparation time: 25 minutes, plus standing and
rising**
Cooking time: 50-65 minutes
Oven: 220°C, 425°F, Gas Mark 7

1. Crumble the yeast into a small bowl. Cream with 1 teaspoon of the sugar, and mix in the tepid water. Leave in a warm place to froth – about 10 minutes.

2. Sift the flour into a bowl and make a well in the centre; add the yeast liquid, the remaining sugar, the melted butter and the beaten egg. Work to a smooth dough.

3. Put the dough into a floured bowl and cover with a damp teatowel or large freezer bag. Leave in a warm place for 1 hour or until doubled in bulk.

4. Knock back the dough and knead in the chopped fruits and almonds.

5. Shape the dough into a large round loaf and place on a greased baking sheet or put the dough into an 18 cm (7 inch) greased brioche tin. Cover again and leave for 40-45 minutes or until doubled in bulk.

6. Bake in a preheated oven for 50-55 minutes, cover with foil once the top of the loaf has browned well. Test with a fine skewer to see that the bread is cooked through, if the skewer does not come out clean, bake the bread for about 10 minutes longer.

7. Cool on a wire tray. **F**

F Can be frozen for up to 6 months. Thaw at room temperature for 4 hours or bake at 150°C, 300°F, Gas Mark 2 for about 40 minutes.

SPAIN

TORTAS DE ACEITE
Aniseed and Sesame Seed Biscuits

Makes about 16
250 ml (8 fl oz) olive oil
2 long strips lemon peel
1 tablespoon aniseed
1 tablespoon sesame seeds
5 tablespoons dry white wine
finely grated rind of ½ lemon
finely grated rind of ½ orange
50 g (2 oz) caster sugar
450 g (1 lb) plain flour
2 teaspoons ground cinnamon
3 tablespoons nibbed or chopped, blanched almonds
1 egg white, beaten

Preparation time: 30 minutes, plus standing and chilling
Cooking time: 23-28 minutes
Oven: 180°C, 350°F, Gas Mark 4

These dry, close-textured biscuits have a typically Spanish flavour.

1. Heat the olive oil in a shallow frying pan over a moderate heat for 2-3 minutes. Remove from the heat and add the lemon peel, aniseed and sesame seeds. Leave to cool completely.
2. Remove the lemon peel and pour the oil and seeds into a large mixing bowl.
3. Stir in the white wine, lemon and orange rind, and caster sugar.
4. Sift together the flour and cinnamon, and beat, little by little, into the wine and oil mixture. If the mixture becomes very stiff, work the dough with your hands.
5. When the dough is smooth, shape it into a neat ball, wrap it in cling film and chill for 30 minutes.
6. Divide the dough into 16 pieces and shape each one by hand into a round flat biscuit.
7. Place the biscuits on lightly greased baking sheets, allowing plenty of room for spreading.
8. Brush the tops of the biscuits with beaten egg white and press a few almond pieces into each one.
9. Place in a preheated oven and bake for 20-25 minutes.
10. Cool on a wire tray. Ⓐ Ⓕ
Ⓐ Can be made up to 3 weeks in advance and stored in an airtight container.
Ⓕ Thaw frozen biscuits for 30 minutes.

SPAIN

PASTEL DE MANZANA
Apple and Mint Pudding

Serves 6
100 g (4 oz) plain flour
½ teaspoon baking powder
175 g (6 oz) caster sugar
25 g (1 oz) ground almonds
1 small egg, beaten
1 tablespoon lemon juice
1 kg (2 lb) cooking apples
2 tablespoons chopped fresh mint (see below)
2 teaspoons ground cinnamon
pouring or single cream, to serve

Preparation time: 25-30 minutes
Cooking time: about 45 minutes
Oven: 180°C, 350°F, Gas Mark 4

This pudding is similar to the traditional apple crumble, except that the crust is hard and crisp. It should have quite a prominent minty flavour, but the quantity of mint can be reduced by as much as a half if preferred.

1. Sift together the flour and baking powder into a mixing bowl. Add the sugar and the ground almonds.
2. Make a well in the centre and pour in the beaten egg.
3. Using 2 forks, work the ingredients into a fairly coarse crumble mixture.
4. Two-thirds fill a large mixing bowl with water and add the lemon juice. Peel, core and thickly slice the apples into the water (to prevent them browning). Drain the apple slices thoroughly and toss them with the chopped mint and cinnamon.
5. Arrange the spiced apple slices in the bottom of a greased 1 litre (1¾ pint) pie dish. Press the crumble mixture evenly on the top.
6. Bake in a preheated oven for about 45 minutes until a rich golden crust has formed.
7. Serve straight from the oven with the cream.

FROM THE TOP Tortas de aceite; Quesadillas

SPAIN

QUESADILLAS
Vanilla Cheese Pastry Squares

Makes 8-10
Pastry:
350 g (12 oz) plain flour
large pinch of salt
½ teaspoon mixed spice
175 g (6 oz) butter
1 egg, beaten
1 egg yolk
4 tablespoons water
Filling:
225 g (8 oz) cottage cheese, sieved or drained (see recipe)
½ teaspoon mixed spice
1 egg
2 egg yolks
50 g (2 oz) currants
50 g (2 oz) flaked almonds
To finish:
milk, for glazing
1 tablespoon vanilla sugar (page 56)

Preparation time: 40 minutes, plus chilling
Cooking time: 20-25 minutes
Oven: 200°C, 400°F, Gas Mark 6

1. To make the pastry, sift the flour, salt and mixed spice into a bowl. Rub in the butter until the mixture resembles fine breadcrumbs.
2. Mix the egg with the egg yolk and the water. Stir into the dry ingredients and work into a smooth dough.
3. Shape the dough into a ball, wrap it in cling film and chill for 30 minutes. Ⓐ
4. Then make the filling. If a textured filling is preferred simply drain the cottage cheese; for a smoother filling push the cottage cheese through a sieve. Stir the mixed spice, egg, egg yolks, currants and almonds into the prepared cottage cheese.
5. Divide the dough in half. Roll out one half and use to line the base of a greased, shallow rectangular tin 18 cm (7 inches) × 28 cm (11 inches), trimming the pastry so that it does not come up the sides of the tin.
6. Spread the cheese filling over the pastry.
7. Roll out the remaining portion of dough and cut it into a rectangle the same size as the tin; place it over the filling.
8. To finish, brush the top with milk and sprinkle with the vanilla sugar.
9. Bake in a preheated oven for 20-25 minutes until lightly golden.
10. Allow to cool and then cut into rectangles or squares.
Ⓐ Dough can be prepared up to 2 days in advance, covered and chilled. Bring back to room temperature and proceed with step 4.

GREECE

HALVA
Semolina and Wine Sweetmeat

Makes about 36 pieces
250 ml (8 fl oz) olive oil
500 g (1¼ lb) fine semolina
450 g (1 lb) sugar
750 ml (1¼ pints) milk
250 ml (8 fl oz) dry Greek white wine
cinnamon, for dusting

Preparation time: 5 minutes, plus chilling
Cooking time: 20-25 minutes

Homemade halva is deliciously soft, unlike the dense halva which can be found in Greek food shops.

FROM THE LEFT Halva; Baklava

1. Heat the oil in a large shallow frying pan over a gentle heat.

2. Pour in the semolina in a fine, steady stream, stirring continuously.

3. Cook gently, stirring from time to time, until all the oil has been absorbed and the semolina is pale golden.

4. Stir in the sugar, milk and white wine. Cook for 10 minutes, stirring continuously, until the mixture is thick and will hold its shape on a wooden spoon (take care that it does not burn).

5. Pour into a lightly greased shallow rectangular dish or tin 20 cm (8 inches) × 30 cm (12 inches) (or use 2 smaller tins if preferred) and level off the surface.

6. Chill for about 4 hours until firm. Ⓐ Dust lightly with cinnamon, cut into squares or rectangles and serve with strong black coffee.

Ⓐ Can be stored, chilled, for up to 3 days.

GREECE
BAKLAVA
Spiced Phyllo Pie

Serves 8-10
225 g (8 oz) butter, melted
20-24 sheets phyllo pastry
225 g (8 oz) shelled pistachio nuts chopped
25 g (1 oz) caster sugar
1 teaspoon ground cinnamon
Syrup:
225 g (8 oz) sugar
150 ml (¼ pint) water
juice and grated rind of ½ lemon
2 tablespoons orange-flower water (see below)
To decorate:
1 tablespoon shelled pistachio nuts, chopped

Preparation time: about 45 minutes, plus chilling
Cooking time: 45-50 minutes
Oven: 180°C, 350°F, Gas Mark 4
then: 220°C, 425°F, Gas Mark 7

Orange-flower water, which adds the characteristic Greek flavour to the syrup, can be bought from most chemists.

1. Brush a rectangular dish 30 cm (12 inches) × 20 cm (8 inches) with the melted butter.
2. Lay half the sheets of phyllo pastry in the dish, brushing the top of each sheet with melted butter as it is laid down.
3. Mix the chopped pistachio nuts or almonds with the sugar and cinnamon and sprinkle over the pastry sheets.
4. Lay the remaining sheets of phyllo pastry on top, brushing each one with melted butter as before.
5. Brush the top of the pie with melted butter.
6. Using a sharp knife, cut lengthways lines in the pastry and cut across these diagonally to make diamond shapes. A
7. For the syrup, put the sugar, water, lemon juice and lemon rind into a pan, and stir over a gentle heat until the sugar has dissolved. Simmer steadily until the syrup is thick enough to coat the back of a spoon.
8. Stir in the orange-flower water and simmer for a further 1-2 minutes.
9. Allow the syrup to cool, then chill in the refrigerator. A
10. Place the baklava in a preheated oven and bake for 30 minutes, then raise the oven temperature and bake for a further 10 minutes until the baklava is puffed and golden. F A
11. Remove from the oven and immediately pour the chilled syrup over. Sprinkle with pistachios and cool.
12. Divide the baklava into portions, along the lines that were cut before baking, and serve.
A The baklava and syrup can be prepared 3-4 days in advance. Keep separate, cover and chill. Alternatively the finished baklava (uncut) can be prepared 3-4 days in advance, covered and chilled until required.
F Freeze cooled baklava without its syrup topping. Reheat from frozen at 190°C, 375°F, Gas Mark 5 for 25-30 minutes. Remove from the oven, prepare the syrup and pour over immediately. Cool.

Phyllo pastry (or filo pastry) is an extremely thin pastry, similar to strudel pastry. It is sold in rolls in Greek shops and delicatessens.
Phyllo is always used several layers at a time and each layer is brushed with melted butter to keep it moist. On baking the layers puff up and become crisp; they also shrink so allow a generous overlap when lining a baking dish.

GREECE

LOUKOUMADES
Yeast and Honey Buns

Makes 20-24
200 g (7 oz) plain flour
½ teaspoon salt
15 g (½ oz) fresh yeast or 2 teaspoons dried yeast
1 teaspoon clear honey
150 ml (¼ pint) milk
25 g (1 oz) butter, melted
oil for deep frying
50 g (2 oz) caster sugar
2 teaspoons ground cinnamon
Sauce:
100 g (4 oz) plain chocolate, broken into small pieces
2 tablespoons clear honey
3 tablespoons lemon juice
50 g (2 oz) unsalted butter
150 ml (¼ pint) water
1 teaspoon cornflour

Preparation time: 40-45 minutes, plus rising
Cooking time: about 12 minutes

1. Sift the flour and salt into a bowl.
2. Crumble the fresh yeast into the honey and mix together well; gradually beat in the milk and the melted butter. If using dried yeast, soak it in half the given quantity of milk and the honey. Leave in a warm place until frothy, then beat in the rest of the milk and the melted butter.
3. Make a well in the sifted flour, pour in the yeast liquid and work to a smooth dough.
4. Divide the dough into 20-24 pieces and mould each one into a small ball.
5. Place the dough balls on a large greased baking sheet, allowing plenty of room for spreading. Leave the baking sheet in a warm place until the dough balls have doubled in size.
6. Meanwhile mix together the sugar and cinnamon.
7. To make the sauce, put the chocolate, honey, lemon juice and butter into a saucepan with 7 tablespoons of the water. Stir over a gentle heat until the chocolate has dissolved.
8. Blend the cornflour to a smooth paste with the remaining water and stir into the chocolate mixture; mix well then stir over a gentle heat until the sauce thickens.
9. Heat the oil in a deep frying pan to 180°C-190°C/350°F-375°F or until a cube of bread browns in 30 seconds. Gently lower batches of dough balls into the pan and fry for 5-7 minutes until golden all over. Drain thoroughly on paper towels and toss immediately in the cinnamon sugar.
10. Serve the loukoumades hot, topped with the re-heated chocolate sauce.

GREECE

RAVANIE
Diamond-shaped Orange Cakes

Serves 8-10
100 g (4 oz) butter, softened
225 g (8 oz) caster sugar
175 g (6 oz) plain flour
2 teaspoons baking powder
pinch of salt
½ teaspoon mixed spice
50 g (2 oz) fine semolina
finely grated rind and juice of 2 oranges
2 eggs
1 tablespoon sesame seeds
Syrup glaze:
100 g (4 oz) sugar
juice and finely grated rind of 1 orange
2 tablespoons clear honey
To decorate:
2 tablespoons sesame seeds
lightly toasted strips of candied orange peel

Preparation time: 30-40 minutes
Cooking time: about 1 hour 20 minutes
Oven: 180°C, 350°F, Gas Mark 4

1. Grease a rectangular tin 25 cm (10 inches) × 18 cm (7 inches) and line with greaseproof paper or non-stick silicone paper.
2. Cream the butter and sugar until pale and fluffy; this can be done by hand, with an electric mixer or in a food processor.
3. Sift together the flour, baking powder, salt and mixed spice. Add to the creamed mixture, together with the semolina, orange rind and juice, eggs and sesame seeds. Mix well until blended.
4. Spread the mixture evenly in the prepared tin and bake in a preheated oven for about 1¼ hours, until firm but spongy to the touch.
5. Meanwhile make the syrup glaze. Put the sugar, orange rind and juice into a pan and stir over a gentle heat until the sugar has dissolved.
6. Add the honey and boil gently for 3 minutes.
7. When the cake is ready, remove it from the oven and pierce it at evenly-spaced intervals with a fine skewer. Spoon the syrup glaze evenly over the top.
8. Sprinkle with the toasted sesame seeds. Leave to cool.
9. Decorate with the strips of candied orange peel. Cut into diamond shapes and serve. Ⓐ
Ⓐ This cake keeps for up to 1 week, covered with foil, in a cool place.

FROM THE LEFT Ravanie; Keskul

GREECE

KESKUL
Almond, Lemon and Pomegranate Custard

Serves 6
450 ml (¾ pint) single cream
450 ml (¾ pint) milk
150 g (5 oz) ground almonds
175 g (6 oz) caster sugar
½ teaspoon almond essence
finely grated rind of ½ lemon
40 g (1½ oz) rice flour or cornflour
3 tablespoons water or milk
To decorate:
2 tablespoons fresh pomegranate seeds or slices of kiwi
   fruit
1 tablespoon shelled pistachio nuts, split lengthways

Preparation time: 20 minutes plus cooling and chilling
Cooking time: 6-8 minutes

1. Put the cream into a pan with the milk and stir in the ground almonds, sugar, almond essence and grated lemon rind.
2. Bring the mixture just to the boil over a gentle heat; remove the pan from the heat, cover with a lid, and allow to cool for 20 minutes.
3. Stand a sieve over a clean saucepan and pour the cooled almond milk through it, pressing the almonds against the sieve to extract their flavour.
4. Stand the pan of strained milk over a gentle heat.
5. Blend the rice flour with the tablespoons of water or milk to a smooth paste; slowly stir in the warmed almond milk.
6. Return the mixture to the pan and stir over a gentle heat until the mixture is thick enough to coat the back of a wooden spoon. (The custard can be sieved at this stage if you want it really smooth.)
7. Spoon the almond custard into 6 individual bowls and chill for 1 hour.
8. Decorate each serving with pomegranate seeds (or slices of kiwi fruit) and pistachio nuts.

MOROCCO

YO-YO
Orange Flavoured Buns

Makes 10-12
225 g (8 oz) plain flour
2 teaspoons bicarbonate of soda
pinch of salt
2 eggs
3 tablespoons olive oil
2 tablespoons orange juice
finely grated rind of 1½ oranges
500 g (1 lb 2 oz) caster sugar
450 ml (¾ pint) water
2 tablespoons lemon juice
175 g (6 oz) honey
oil, for deep frying

Preparation time: 40-45 minutes, plus rising
Cooking time: 20-25 minutes

1. Sift the flour, bicarbonate of soda and salt into a large bowl and make a well in the centre.
2. Beat the eggs with the olive oil, orange juice, half the grated orange rind and 50 g (2 oz) of the caster sugar.
3. Add the egg and orange mixture to the sifted ingredients and beat to a thick batter; it should fall from the back of a wooden spoon in a thick ribbon.

4. Cover the bowl with a clean, damp teatowel and leave to rise in a warm place for about 30 minutes or until doubled in bulk.
5. To make the syrup, put the remaining 450 g (1 lb) sugar into a pan with the water and lemon juice. Stir over a gentle heat until the sugar has dissolved.
6. Bring to the boil and cook over a brisk heat until the syrup reaches 110°C/230°F, on a sugar thermometer or when a little dropped from a spoon on to a saucer forms a thick thread.
7. Stir in the honey and remaining orange rind and simmer for 4-5 minutes. Remove from the heat and cover.
8. Heat the oil in a deep frying pan to 180°-190°C/350°-375°F or when a cube of bread browns in 30 seconds.
9. With well-floured hands, work the dough into a ball and divide into 10-12 even-sized pieces. Shape 3-4 pieces at a time into balls and then press a finger through the centre of each one to make a ring doughnut shape.
10. Deep fry 3-4 buns at a time, for about 5 minutes, turning them once. Drain thoroughly on paper towels. Shape and fry the remaining dough pieces, 3-4 at a time.
11. Prick each cooked bun at regular intervals with a fine skewer. Using a draining spoon, dip each doughnut into the warm syrup and allow the excess to drip off. Arrange on a serving dish and serve immediately with the remaining syrup.

FRANCE

TARTE AUX PRUNEAUX À L'ARMAGNAC
Prune and Ground Almond Flan

Serves 6
175 g (6 oz) rich shortcrust pastry
225 g (8 oz) pitted prunes
6 tablespoons Armagnac
2 eggs
6 tablespoons double cream
40 g (1½ oz) vanilla sugar (page 56)
finely grated rind of ½ orange
3 tablespoons ground almonds
40 g (1½ oz) butter, melted

Preparation time: 20 minutes, plus chilling and marinating
Cooking time: about 25 minutes
Oven: 200°C, 400°F, Gas Mark 6

This is one of the best pastry desserts to come from the South of France. 'Tartes' abound in this area of the Mediterranean, but none of them quite match the rich flavour and creaminess of Tarte aux Pruneaux.

1. Roll out the pastry quite thinly and line a 20 cm (8 inch) loose-bottomed flan tin, pressing the pastry up the sides well.
2. Chill the flan case for 1 hour. Ⓐ
3. Meanwhile put the pitted prunes into a bowl, pour the Armagnac over and leave to stand for 1 hour. Ⓐ
4. Drain the prunes well, reserving the brandy.
5. Arrange the prunes over the base of the chilled flan case.
6. Beat the eggs with the cream, then mix in the vanilla sugar, orange rind, ground almonds and melted butter.
7. Pour the egg and cream mixture into the flan case over the prunes.
8. Bake in a preheated oven for about 25 minutes, until the filling is golden and slightly puffed. Ⓕ
9. Remove from the oven, spoon over the reserved Armagnac, and serve immediately with single cream.
Ⓐ Flan case and prunes can be prepared up to 1 day in advance. Keep separate, cover and chill.
Ⓕ Reheat from frozen at 150°C, 300°F, Gas Mark 2.

INDEX